# TALES FROM
# THE BLUE LINE

# Dear You,

by Chyana Marie Sage

*For every person who has ever*
*had their trust or love taken advantage of—*
*I'm so sorry you had to go through that.*
*I'm here with you & one day you will heal.*

*I hope my words*
*can be apart of your healing journey.*

*Crimespree Magazine Presents*

# TALES FROM THE BLUE LINE

ROB RILEY

DOWN&OUT
BOOKS

Down & Out Books
3959 Van Dyke Rd, Ste. 265
Lutz, FL 33558
www.DownAndOutBooks.com

Cover art and design by JT. Lindroos

ISBN: 1937495957
ISBN-13: 978-1-937495-95-4

*To my Brothers' in Blue*

The fine police officers I encountered and worked with during my career. They were a dedicated and courageous group of people, putting their lives on the line every day they were on the street.

The unavoidable controversies of the profession also occurred during our time. For facing the adversity, they all deserve an extra medal for bravery in the field.

# ONE
## *O.J. Simpson*

The O.J. Simpson drama provided this country with more overall, inside information on how the legal system works—from cops up to judges—than, in my not so humble opinion, all of the previous cases in history combined.

I'm not speaking merely of how the laws were created, developed and enacted from the country's beginning. Nor the uncountable cases started by law breakers and then dispatched either by not being processed or someone's life ending on the gallows. Of course, one must at least consider the unknowable broken laws that have simply been ignored by everyone who potentially had a say in the matter.

The reason I make my claim is because by the time Mr. Simpson's murder trial was held in 1995, the mass media—especially the visuals provided by television—had entered the stage and elbowed its way squarely into the middle. Sight is the most important of the senses. There's nothing like actually *seeing* things happen. When you're right there, on the spot. The impressions gathered from those moments are not simply the first in line for influencing people, they also work their way into the deepest part of your consciousness.

And they never leave, even if you make your peace with them.

That's what got O.J. off the hook: the people in charge of displaying and interpreting the images accomplished the next part of a person absorbing an observation. They *interpreted* said observations.

The people who wanted O.J. to be found not guilty had more power and influence than those who wanted to convict him of murder. The truth was not part of the equation. That happens all the time in jury trials; now everyone in the world who cared, were able to see how the process works, in person.

But it was twelve people—the jury—who made the decision. Of course. Millions of people saw the trial and had the opportunity to interpret their observations for themselves, to arrive at their own personal conclusions. However, they had no power to affect the outcome.

No group this large had ever collectively witnessed—how things actually work.

People had never in their wildest dreams conceived of a judge, like the one appointed to hear the O.J. trial, who was beyond incompetent. The judge was like someone in a script on *Laugh In*. Late night comedy shows mocked him nightly. Jay Leno had a special judge segment at the beginning of each episode. And if anything, they let the judge off easy. Most likely because the show's writers weren't experts and could not see *all* of the things he was doing wrong.

The horror of the final outcome rests directly on his shoulders. Early on he allowed things to be so out of control that he should have been removed from the case. But the California legal system obviously took no such action. In fact, many of those in a position to assess him were quite possibly just as incompetent as he.

It would have been embarrassing to remove him, to be certain. But leaving him on the bench made things incalculably worse.

The defense attorneys took flat out evil actions to sway the case in their favor. Strong, reliable information suggests one of the defense lawyers was chosen specifically for his ability to estimate the intelligence of potential jurors. A nationally known defense attorney in Milwaukee laughingly told people—I was one of them—that the first thing he looked for in a potential juror during jury selection was how dumb they were. They were the ones he wanted on the jury, so he could work his magic and fool said dummy into believing that a guilty person was innocent. Or that at least there wasn't enough evidence to convict his—guilty—client and perhaps result in a hung jury.

A hung jury is virtually the same as a not guilty verdict for the defense.

The odds against retrying a case and getting a conviction are astronomical—if the presiding District Attorney even decides to make such an attempt. After all, tax payers foot the bill for criminal trials. Try telling them, "We were too incompetent to get a conviction with the first trial. How's about paying for a second trial?" Then ask the taxpayer how much they'd feel like re-electing the D.A. making the request, the next time he or she ran for office.

Lesser issues such as these were never even discussed during the O.J. trial, but they weighed extremely heavy with the people who were affected. The O.J. Simpson trial only needed to give explicit evidence of how larger issues work. The perpetrators of getting a guilty guy off didn't even need a judge as bad as the one handling their case—he was an add on. A far more spectacular add on than anyone had dared dream. Just achieve the goal of what is known as jury nullification, which is having at least one person on the jury who can be manipulated into voting not guilty—no matter how compelling the real evidence—and your client is acquitted.

He walks. To the golf course, where he says, "I'm baaa-ack!" Smiling at his fellow golfers. And at the cameras. And at everyone in the world who was shown enough to believe he'd gotten away with murder.

Nothing like this had ever happened before. The blatant, laugh-in-your-face release of a murderer, where everyone had the chance to watch every day of the massacre being made of the judicial system.

And there was nothing to be done. The system and the traditions of how the court system is allowed to be abused by devious and unscrupulous attorneys and incompetent court authorities was seen live on TV.

And the follow up images, forever on display...The blank-faced, dead-in-the-eye judge sitting on the case let the defense get away with every tactic imaginable. Allowing the years old and undeniably inadmissible interview of an investigating detective by an author on a wholly unrelated subject, where the detective said the "N" word. It was supposed to show that if a police detective ever said the "N" word, the prosecution's entire case was bogus. And it worked! That tape was the hammer that pounded the inevitable not guilty verdict into the chest of the public. The spike was the bloody glove that "doesn't fit," as the defendant himself was allowed to say directly to the jury. Not to mention the worldwide live audience watching on TV.

The bloody glove. Now that wasn't a dirty trick being pulled off by the defense. The prosecutors—the one who ended up crying on another prosecutor's shoulder during an interview immediately after the acquittal—pulled that one off. He was one hundred percent in control of whether the dried up ball of formerly blood-soaked leather was allowed to be pried open and placed on someone's hand.

Now, informed members of the watching world—which was almost all of them—were screaming "leather shrinks after it's been soaked in liquid and then dries out!" Well, there's no way of knowing whether everyone everywhere said those exact words while screaming at their TV screens, but you get the picture.

Since it was the glove that was reasonably considered to be the one worn while the killer committing the crime, everyone knew it would be—what? *It would have shrunk and been too effing small!*

But the veteran prosecuting attorney allowed him to put it on his hand during the court proceeding. And let him say to the world that the glove didn't fit ergo he wasn't the killer. All the elements of yet another *Laugh In* style play on the *Tonight Show* were in place: a dingbat judge drafted from witless members of the L.A. legal community, a dingbat jury crafted by defense attorneys with no conscience and a dingbat prosecutor horribly mishandling critical murder trial evidence on live TV.

You could almost hear O.J. Simpson yelling *I'm baaa-ack!* before the court clerk began reading the not guilty verdict, handed over by the jury foreman.

And so it goes, as newscaster Linda Ellerbee said after each national news broadcast she'd delivered. A relatively sheltered nation glued to the TV, in the same situation as a 2nd grader suddenly being shown hardcore pornography, got a very large dose of at what can happen when the teacher isn't looking.

# TWO
## Origins

When I review my early life I see no clues as to why I became a police officer. Not one. A writer? Yes. A cop? Never. I was unfocused and disorganized, spending all my time dreaming of doing anything other than what I was supposed to be doing. Attention Deficit Disorder hadn't been discovered—some argue invented—but when I read the descriptions of the affliction, I was reminded of a cheerful, yet disinterested younger me.

The fact that I became a hard-boiled detective in adulthood is one for the books...quite literally. I learned early on during my serious writing instruction that clever sayings have a short life before becoming clichés; something people want to neither hear nor be near.

These returning thoughts are written now as a way to display my past...my beginning.

By the time most graduating high school students with modest GPAs hit the streets, they are the newly constructed mold of what we expect to see: an unimpressive tool-like creature, plodding around the neighborhood in search of purpose. On occasion we are surprised, and on even more rare occasions, we surprise ourselves. It was one of these rare occasions when I surprised myself, and everyone who knew me, by becoming a police aide for the Milwaukee Police Department in 1969.

Being around on-duty policemen was an eye opener. No shock there—I was smart enough to know that everything I'd been doing had been wrong. They were all organized, responsible people who were doing an extremely important job. Something awoke in me—a part I didn't know I had. It was a sense of responsibility. Emulating these men was easy for me, and I started right away. Doing the relatively mundane office work of stoking paper reports into aged, creaky metal cabinets led to occasionally answering phone calls from citizens. I found I didn't just enjoy it—I was good at it. The captain of the 7th Precinct in Milwaukee told me so. He told me I had brainpower.

In 1971, at age twenty-one, I was promoted to the formerly called rank of patrolman. On went the blue uniform for a few months while I walked a beat and rode quietly along with senior officers in marked police squad cars.

Then off came the uniform and on went the so-called hippie apparel worn by certain members of society at that time. My short hair grew quickly, hanging past my shoulders in a ragged mess. A patchy beard sprouted on my extremely boyish face and I was scooted to the dark, back rooms of the narcotics squad.

I was undercover. A narc. Revered and respected by many of my fellow officers and hated to a dangerous degree by the element of society I was now assigned to infiltrate. I would spend my days and nights looking to score dope on the streets, cursing The Man during protest marches, and loitering the increasingly dangerous streets of Milwaukee.

I was in.

I spent seven years undercover before returning to uniform for a short while to regain sanity. Then it was back to the narcotics squad where, thanks to many crazy incidents, I would collect the stories and experiences necessary to write my novels. One incident in particular sticks out in my mind...

I was sent to a house in a very bad neighborhood

where heroin was being sold. An informant had introduced me to the main dealer. There was a constant stream of purchasers coming and going. Two narcotics detectives, dressed in regular street clothes, were assigned to cover me while I made the purchase. They parked about a block away in an old junker car. I went to the rear door, knocked and was led into the hallway by a dark-natured dude. The kitchen door opened and a few people in the room strained to get a good look at me. When they stopped and relaxed, the dealer sold me heroin. Simple as that.

This was the 1970s—there were no microphones taped to my chest—or any other body part, which is a story for another time—nor was there any radio contact. I had no gun. I had no badge. I merely had my raggedy hair partially covering my blanched face and meek smile. Oh, and the twenty-five bucks it cost to buy the drugs. I was alone with no means of contacting the people who were covering me.

After returning to the car—and believe me, these two detectives looked like hippies themselves—I handed over the drug evidence and explained the details of the purchase. I then asked: "Exactly how was it that you were 'covering' me?"

The passenger dick smiled while turning to look at me and said, "Our job is to call the regular cops and seal off the crime scene if you're murdered. We then make sure the police photographer gets good shots of your corpse. We then call the Medical Examiner to convey you to the morgue."

He turned back to the front. "That's our job. What da ya think?" He and his partner, and then believe it or not I, started laughing uproariously.

At age twenty-nine I was promoted to detective and spent the next twenty-two years investigating major crimes. Short hair, suit and tie, the whole clichéd deal. I lived a normal off-duty life with my wife and two children; everything I could hope for. Yet, there was something missing.

A seed planted in my earliest childhood days began sprouting and taking over my consciousness. I wanted to expand my writing from formal police reports to that of the fiction I had been reading. I started with short stories. Quickly, the belief that I could write novels pushed the short story thing out of the way. I took some short story correspondence courses and got nothing published. Some gracious and patient instructors taught me the rules not every novice has the luck of learning.

In my early forties I reached out and began a thirteen-year novel writing class. Six novels later—none of them published—and I was beginning to question my path. My instructor, who quickly became one of the best friends I've ever had, ordered me not to give up and quit. He looked me in the eye and said I should see him as my police captain who was giving me a direct order.

"You've got what it takes to sell novels," he constantly encouraged.

Since I was enjoying myself and receiving encouragement from my teacher and fellow students, I stuck with it. I started with horror fiction—an interest arising from my profound childhood love of Edgar Alan Poe. I was still a cop and doing police fiction would have been what they used to call a bus man's holiday—spending your off time to write about your career. I never considered it.

When I was fifty I retired from the police force after thirty-two years of service. Coincidentally—or not, if you believe in fate—I read *The Big Sleep* by Raymond Chandler—an iconic, best-selling crime mystery writer from the 1930s through the 1950s. I was mesmerized. Not only because of the great story telling, but the style. The so-called noir-esque style of the cynical, not-boundby-the-law private detective being written about during that era: Chandler, Dashiell Hammett, Mickey Spillane and others.

I loved everything about these stories. The detectives: Philip Marlowe by Chandler, Sam Spade by Hammett and Mike Hammer by Spillane. Not to mention their dames with soft shoulders and loose legs and the bad guys who possessed many of the same personality traits as the PI's. The darkness of it all...chilling... overwhelming. To me, anyway.

I became a crime mystery fiction writer, using the first person style, a la Raymond Chandler, to delineate the mess of a life of Jack Blanchard: a former Milwaukee Police Detective who quit the force in a huff to become a private investigator and get away from the stupid politics, slime ball crooks and witless bosses. Though, with any good detective story, we know the minute you request a quiet life is the moment things become truly interesting...I guess not all detective stories are fiction.

# THREE
## *Mary*

"I'm famous," the short old woman, wearing a thick scarf and a long, worn out overcoat said.

She was standing straight, but leaning slightly against a concrete street light pole. It was dark. It was cold. Too cold outside for an old woman to be standing motionless for any length of time, even if her head was covered, and she was wearing a worn out overcoat.

"That's not what I asked you," I said, standing behind her.

Cars whirred past on South Kinnickinnic Avenue, in a section of Milwaukee known as Bay View. Some of them slowed, their passengers straining to look at the woman and me. Tiny snowflakes flitted past the overhead street lamp and then out of sight, the way they always do when it's snowing at night. But they were falling. Falling onto me in my blue, winter police uniform and onto the famous old lady standing before me.

She did not respond. I touched her lightly on the shoulder. "Are you alright, ma'am?" I asked.

She was not all right. The smell of alcohol wafted from her to me, in unpleasant waves. She was, in fact, drunk. Hammered would be the better word.

She'd been standing this way since I'd first seen her, about a block and a half away, while I was walking my police beat. I walked straight to her. She didn't move an inch. While trying to communicate with her, a couple of somewhat sober men approached. They'd been in the tavern a few doors away. I heard yelling inside the tavern while one of the men held the door open. A small group of men squeezed together to stare out the window at the odd scene.

A lighted Pabst Blue Ribbon beer decoration slipped from the window. The men who'd been standing there scuttled away and now there was yelling and swearing coming from inside the tavern—didn't need the door open to hear it.

"Purse!" the woman shouted. Large drops of spit flew from her mouth when she spoke.

"She wants you to look in her purse," one of the now-annoying men said while the small group inched toward me. A couple of them started laughing.

The old woman was standing still, her forehead seemingly glued to the pole. She was more than just drunk.

She was blotto.

I ignored the men and slid the purse from her shoulder. She leaned to let it slide off and then amazingly righted herself. She was a professional drunkard; one who could still handle slight movements before they finally caved in and fell to their inevitable dark stupor.

She'd obviously been through this before.

"She's been doing this stuff for long as I remember," one of the men said. "Drinkin' all night and stumbling out here."

I looked at him. "And you've been helping her as long as you remember, too," I said.

I was a twenty-three-year-old police officer, but I'd quickly learned the sarcastic tone one must take in order to let potential trouble makers know you were on their case.

The man stepped back, lowered his head and raised his hands. He was a good boy, been around cops dealing with drunks for a long time. Undoubtedly he was one of those drunks on some occasions. But he knew his place when a police officer uttered a wise remark. And that was walking backward with your head down, arms up, and most importantly, your mouth shut. His comrades held out their arms and embraced him when he returned to their pack. They all moved together, shuttling away from the woman and me.

I began looking through the woman's purse. Usual stuff: make-up equipment, a couple of pens and a smaller, clasp purse. No wallet.

"Paper," the woman said, while attempting to turn toward me. She began to fall. I caught her but we both went down to the sidewalk.

I stood and pulled her to her feet. She was small and not too heavy. But she had that mushy feel that all inactive people have and the odor of alcohol burst into my face when she coughed. I managed to prop her against the light pole and stood close to prevent her—and me, damn it—from falling again.

She groaned as she tried to speak. I waited. Looking up at the streetlight, I could tell the snow was falling more heavily. Damn! I started digging into her purse again, looking for identification. While digging I noticed her take a breath, hold it, and lean toward me.

"Newspaper in the purse," she shouted. It had taken all her energy to speak.

She was blotto plus.

Newspaper in the messy purse? What the hell...

A folded, yellowed and flimsy piece of old newspaper was tucked into her coin purse. Nothing else—certainly no coins, or money in any form, just the relatively neatly folded newspaper clipping.

"Ha!" she shouted when she saw I'd found it. She was grinning...sneering.

While beginning to unfold the paper I sensed a man

walking toward us. He was coming from the direction of the tavern. He was nimble and stepped quickly. He was not drunk. I was glad.

"Excuse me, Officer," the man said, and stopped several steps away from me. He was being respectful. Polite. I kept my guard up, anyway.

"Yeah," I said, looking at him.

"That's Mary," he said. He was wearing a heavy coat with a fur-lined hood, which he kept down from his head. He was balding, graying, average height and build.

"Yeah?" I said again, with a slight tone in my voice.

"She's got that old newspaper clipping," the man said. "Carries it everywhere. Especially for stuff like this."

Stuff like what? I did not ask.

I looked back at the newspaper clipping, which was quite old and flimsy, and saw the large, dark print at the heading: Woman Saves Family From Fire.

I didn't need to read the accompanying article to figure out what was going on.

"'Bout ten years ago she was walking to her then-favorite tavern, couple blocks from here," the man continued. "Smelled and then saw smoke coming from the window of a house. It was dark and late, so she went up and pounded on the door. Screamed and yelled. Neighbors heard and looked out their windows, called the police."

The man had memorized the story he was telling. I checked the clipping and saw verifying words in the story.

"She lives a block from here," the man said, pointing across the street. "Go through that yard and her basement flat is right there."

I thanked the man. "I own this place," he said, pointing at the tavern behind him. "Stop in next time you're on this beat. We'll have a beer. Or something a little more, if you want."

"Thanks," I said while gathering Mary and her purse and her newspaper story.

"Lotsa' coppers have walked her home from places around here over the years. They all know her. She shows that news clipping to the new guys, so they don't throw her in jail."

I was definitely a new guy; my first time on this particular beat. And this was definitely the most unusual thing I had come upon. Bay View was a fairly tame, family-friendly area, even at night.

Mary had gathered some strength and began to move. I put one hand in her armpit and held on tightly. The street was clear of cars and we started walking across. She'd gained energy and was doing fairly well. Her balance failed her a couple of times, but walking with her was easier than I thought it would be.

We finished the block-long trek and approached her home. It wasn't what I'd call a home, but she was obviously limited. Her abode was in the back of the building and after going down the concrete steps leading to an old wooden door that was barely six feet high, she grunted while pulling away from me and pushed open the door. The house beyond was completely dark and the odor of household neglect wafted out.

It was snowing heavier than ever and my nice blue uniform was turning white with snowflakes.

I felt good, walking back toward Kinnickinnic Avenue. I mean, here was this poor old woman who was obviously drinking herself into a grave, who badly needed medical attention, but I'd managed to help her. Saved her from falling and freezing in the street that night, or worse. It was a moment in time, a moment where I felt as though I'd done one of the most important things a policeman can do.

# FOUR
*Strakowski*

Carl didn't like new guys comin' to the crib. Didn't like it at all.

When I knocked on the door I was expecting to see his brother, Eddie. Carl was too high to deal at night. That's what my reliable, drug addicted police informant had told me. Go figure.

"Wha's your name?" he asked while I stood in his door way. It *was* late: 8:00 p.m.

His basement living quarters were a dimly lit mess. Typical of those that littered most of the tall, early 20th century homes that stood about fifteen feet apart in the sagging, south side neighborhood.

The doorway was shorter than a man six feet tall; like me. I had to stoop to get a better look at Carl. He'd clearly intended to keep me from entering, squaring himself off before me in a defiant manner. The look in his eyes was defiance plus: the plus being hatred and the glaze of someone high on heroin. No doubt he'd been high all day.

"That Joe?" I heard Eddie yell from the other side of the basement. "He's been here before!"

I stood on the stairway, watching Carl, listening to the voice from the dark behind him.

Carl didn't know me. Eddie had been there the first time I showed up with my police informant, Ray, and bought heroin from him. Ray had been taking me—a long-haired, bearded, undercover cop—into one of the hottest dope dens in the city of Milwaukee. This time I had gone alone to visit, with no appointment.

My commanding officer was eager to get heroin delivery cases on all of the dealers living at Carl's place as soon as possible. He was happy to have me take big risks.

Carl had been slouching and was a bit wobbly. He straightened and looked toward the other side of the basement. He stared for an uncomfortably long time. He shook his head and grumbled unintelligible words. Then he looked at me.

He was not happy.

I cautiously stepped down the creaking wooden stairs and followed when Carl shrugged and walked toward a small wooden table shoved against the wall to my left.

Eddied had probably talked me up to Carl, but Carl hadn't expected to see me. He obviously hated surprises. Being a heroin dealer, certain surprises could land him in prison for ten to twenty.

I followed him to the table, straining to see anyone in the dark rear part of the basement...no luck.

"No noddin', dude," Carl said to a large young man who was deeply slouched in an old kitchen chair near the table. He'd been sunk so low I hadn't seen him. Carl stepped toward the snoozing big man and kicked him in the leg...hard. He had to. The big man had just shot up and had the reaction time of a corpse.

The young man obviously wasn't in with the regular cabal of addicts who visited this particular den. Only regulars got to stay after doing their bag.

I looked more closely at him while he stirred and pushed himself up from the chair. He wore a dark knit hat pulled down to his eyebrows and a filthy green army jacket. Something was familiar. Suddenly I recognized him. Ah! He'd been an all-city tackle in high school. I had also played football in high school. I remembered his face from his photo in the sports section of the local newspaper. He still looked like his photo in the sports section of the newspaper. I'd studied those photos when the paper came out. I'd been envious.

The football star-turned-junkie had been given a football scholarship by the University of Wisconsin when he graduated from high school. This was no longer that star.

It was a sad, watershed moment for me, among the first—and most dreary—of my police career.

The big junkie roused himself a little more, stood, and walked straight to the exit. No thank yous or good-byes could be heard. Just an unspoken *Get the fuck out.*

Carl looked at me inquisitively.

I said, "Three."

He raised his hand over his head, with three fingers sticking up. A dark figure on the other side of the basement stood and moved toward a side room. Eddie! A moment later Eddie came out and walked toward us. He smiled, with droopy, unfocused eyes.

"What up, bro?" he asked, unable to raise his head high enough to look at my face. But he *knew* me. Good for him.

I was "Joe."

Eddied handed three small foil packets to Carl, who took them and looked at me.

"Three for a quarter?" he asked.

"Yeah." Three for a quarter meant three ten-dollar bags of product for twenty-five bucks. I always marveled at the unique turns of phrase created by street thugs, dopers and the like.

He gave me the three bags.

I gave him a twenty and a five. He grabbed them without looking at me or saying anything.

It was my turn to get the fuck out.

Which I did, and quickly. I had my buy in my tight fist and was headed back to the narcotics detectives who were covering me, where they'd parked their vehicle two blocks away.

Four days later I reported for duty at the narcotics squad.

"Hi, ya, killer," Detective Lee said to me as I walked through the door. He was a wide man with a big belly and a big laugh. "The Bureau's checkin' you out; see if you're an accomplice." He sat back in his chair, behind the desk that stood a few feet away from the entrance of the room.

I stopped in place and smiled back at him. I had no idea what he was talking about.

Killer? Bureau? In the parlance of the Milwaukee Police Department, that meant the Detective Bureau—where the homicide squad was.

I felt my face turn hot and the red glow that was growing on my cheeks.

"You're supposed to be on the run. Everyone else from 6th Street is."

Carl and Eddie lived on 6th Street. Their place had its own name. Everyone who did drug investigations in the city knew what you meant when you said, "The place on 6th Street." Carl and Eddie's house of heroin.

Bill "Donuts" D'Amato came to the room from the hallway behind me.

"Okay, Lee," he said to Detective Lee. "Tell the kid what's really up. No bullshit."

"You were 'made' the other day," the detective said. "A guy in back—name of Dennis Strakowski—knew you from Junior High School...knew your name was Robin Riley...had heard you'd became a cop."

"He didn't say anything." Stating the obvious is normal when you're in a state of shock.

"Guess he was stunned. Figured there might be more cops right outside the door. After you left he told Carl and Eddie who you really were."

"So why am I on the run?'" I asked. "You guys aren't gonna protect me?" I chuckled, trying to appear hip and play along with the joke being played on me. Ha ha, and all that.

"Strakowski and other guys—we know it was Carl and Eddie, but can't prove it—went to Ray's crib last night," Lee said.

"To get even with 'em?" I interrupted. "What—and someone says I was *with* 'em"?

"Just a joke, ya little shit," Detective Lee said. "Calm down."

"Ray's wife was at work, and Ray was home babysitting their infant," Detective Lee continued. "A neighbor across the hall saw three guys go in—they're all still on the run—and leave about a half hour later. He heard the baby crying and crying. Went in and found Ray dead...laying on the floor. Some empty heroin bags and street needles were on the table, in plain sight. Arranged, like as a message for whoever found him. You know, snitch to the cops and they're gonna kill ya."

"The dude's been ID'd?" I asked.

"Workin' on it. But the homicide squad's been digging, and some of the people who were there when you scored your dope have been talked to and one of them gave up Strakowski's name. He, Carl and Eddie fit the descriptions of the guys who came to Rays' place."

We were all silent for a long moment.

"And...?" I asked.

"Don't look good," Donuts said. "The witness never saw their faces. Claims he never got that good 'a look."

The coroner had quickly confirmed the cause of death: massive heroin overdose with a single fresh injection site. What they call a Hot Shot in the streets.

All three of Ray's visitors that night eventually showed up at homes of relatives. Never gave statements

23

to the police. Never got charged with Ray's murder...or any crime.

Ray's wife told one of the investigating detectives she was glad it was all over with. She could take her kid and go home to her mother's.

The other guys in the narcotics office went to their desks. Same old, same old.

Except for me, the new guy. A huge increment of change had invaded my head space. I didn't like it.

# FIVE
## *The Stones*

Milwaukee County Stadium was the modest housing of a major league baseball team, the Milwaukee Brewers. Built in 1953, it initially housed the former Boston Braves, who moved that year to Milwaukee for a cup of coffee and then fled town to Atlanta in 1965. The Green Bay Packers of the NFL played three games there every season, from 1955 until 1994.

The place was torn down and replaced in 2000. That describes an extremely short lived sports arena.

But it was more than a sports arena.

The 1970s, America's original "Me Decade," also saw the invasion of County Stadium by a bunch of not-so-sporty groups, who were there to be watched and worshiped by an extremely different kind of audience.

I'm referring to Rock 'n Roll bands. The most famous bands in the history of the world began doing gigs at County Stadium—as they had been doing for some time at other outdoor sports coliseums across the country. Fans of said bands literally went crazy over these groups, in a way sports fans never did for their favorite teams. Or for *any* teams, or groups, or whatever. I am certain of this.

Literally crazy? Yes. And I was there, along with my too-small band of fellow undercover police officers, to witness—and spoil—the parties.

Spoiling *parties*? Yes. Drug parties—held by some in the audience—the likes of which cannot be imagined. You had to see 'em to believe 'em.

These were among the largest, most out-of-control drug parties ever held. And none of them was more dopey than those in the so-called hippie oriented sections of the gatherings at the outdoor stadium rock concerts.

The first bust out rock concert at County Stadium was performed by the Rolling Stones in 1974, on a stage erected in front of the center field bleachers. The first County Stadium rock concert drug arrest was made by an undercover cop who bought an ounce of marijuana from a guy in the back seat of a taxi cab, in the parking lot outside the stadium.

The drug arrests. How I wish that was the only type of arrest we officers of the Milwaukee Police Department and the deputies of the Milwaukee County Sheriff's Department, needed to make.

Those were easy. Seize the illegal drug, handcuff the prisoner and then walk him/her to the stadium's command office. Do reports. Go back out to the expansive upper and lower decks and the infield and outfield where the best viewing locations were. Repeat.

That was all daytime stuff, the time when the warm up bands were warming up the crowd. As it grew darker in the sky and drunker in parts of the crowd—or should I say druggier?—the rules changed. Some of the boys and girls wanted more and harder inebriants, which made them harder to arrest.

Fights broke out.

Yes, I said *fights broke out.*

This was our first operation of this kind. As the warm-up bands finished and the Rolling Stones were about to take the stage, the attitude of some in the crowd changed from wanting to get to the music, to wanting to get to their dealers. As in drug dealers. And fast. And they did. They swilled and smoked and injected their intoxicants of choice, and grew from a silly crowd of playground kids, to a dark chamber of maniacs. And that was when our commanding officers, safe in the upper level broadcast booths with their theater glasses, saw and directed us to the worst of the offenders.

Thanks, guys.

I made a drug buy—LSD, or so the dealer claimed—near the third base line. I walked away and my backups moved in to arrest the offender. Then the offenders backups moved in to defend him from the po-lice. They were drunk and full of mindless violence which they were eager to provide to anyone who tried stopping their fun. And it worked.

Three plainclothes, hippie looking officers with me were injured. I grabbed the prisoner and continued walking away. A second gang of fun loving concert goers just outside the third base dugout saw his hands cuffed behind his back. I was holding his arm. Guess what happened?

I ducked and let go of the erstwhile prisoner. I crawled on my hands and knees to get away, while those in the crowed who'd seen who I was began kicking me. In the side. In the ass. In the face. I got up and ran. A bunch of them chased after me. (I'd love to say Mick Jagger was singing the Stones' hit song "Sympathy For The Devil," at the time, but...)

I managed to escape and ran to the police headquarters under the lower deck. My prisoner was—surprise!—sitting in the room. Some uniformed officers had, unbeknownst to me, seen all the fun taking place and jumped in to rescue the undercover narcs I'd left behind. They managed to make some additional arrests and located a guy who was running around with his hands cuffed behind his back. The same one who had sold me a few small squares of paper with drops of some damn dark liquid on them and had then slipped away when the crowd went after me. The pieces of paper were not—ta da!—LSD. But it was common LSD presentation and easy to copy by phony drug dealers who were delivering it to unsuspecting and/or seriously intoxicated members of the crowd. Or narcs who were taking no chances and seizing the product at first sight.

I had rather moderate bruises and a bloody nose. Not bad. I got patched up and went back out to the baseball field. By now the fans were standing and screaming while the Stones played on. Now barely noticed, we undercovers took dope smokers and dealers away from the edge of the crowd. When we returned to the field after processing them, we stood and watched. Some uniformed and plainclothes officers were fighting with resisting offenders in the upper deck. Others were fighting with resisters in the lower deck. And, of course, on the ball field itself. And then we started arresting drug violators once again.

And the band played on.

Once they were really loaded, many music lovers started dancing. They danced on the pitcher's mound. They danced on all three base areas. Some boys pulled out their business and pissed where they stood. No one cared. More than one couple engaged in sexual acts in front of everyone. No one cared. No one was arrested for it, either; no cops were chasing them. By that time it was beyond the Apocalypse.

Large sections of the crowd eventually did everything there was to do. And then they did some more. And then they puked, passed out, came to and dragged their mangy butts to the exits, when they were able to find them.

I told the captain that one guy tried to make a suicide squeeze play at home plate. Which wasn't so bad, but he was in the upper deck at the time.

The captain laughed, told me to shut up—it *was* a B.S. story—and get back to work.

But by that time it was all we had left: crack a few jokes, wonder what the heck we were doing there any longer and finally, prepare to leave.

It must be noted that many in the crowd were well-behaved and disgusted with what the bad actors were doing.

During the next few years there were more open air concerts at County Stadium: Pink Floyd, Heart, The Eagles, Ted Nugent—that's right, *that* Ted Nugent—and on and on. You could look them up.

But the major league baseball players and the umpires complained about the smell of urine in the infield. What was that all about? And the papers reported the number of teenagers who came home smashed on who-knew-what intoxicants. Some teenagers didn't come home for a day or two.

Eventually, the back rooms at Milwaukee's City Hall and the Milwaukee County Executives' office began to rumble with the sound of citizens complaining about the parties for the drugged up, hedonistic fiends being held in the midst of our fine city a few times a year—with the backing and the applause of the news media, politicians, and the business people who stood to make a buck off the deal.

I left the narcotics squad in the late 1970s, with more than a half dozen of these events under my belt. I heard that the Milwaukee County Sheriff's Department took over exclusive law enforcement coverage of the concerts, and that a better system of screening entrants and activities among the crowd was developed.

County Stadium was demolished in 2001. Some say the rock concerts made it old before its time. It sure made it different, on a handful of Saturdays throughout those years.

# SIX
## *Rot-Gut Booze*

I was devastated. It was a warm, Sunday afternoon, in the middle of summer at about 5:00 p.m I was riding around with a man almost twice my age in a dark sedan on Milwaukee's south side. We were relatively quiet, with the older man asking me mundane questions about my life. Slouched in my seat, I gave dull answers in a mostly monotone voice. I was a cop. A newly promoted police detective and I was depressed.

Ingrate?

Not so fast. Or, "Not so much," as they say it these days.

Less than a week earlier I'd worn my hair down past my shoulders and had a face with a full if-mostly-patchy beard. Wore blue jeans and lame T-shirts with words like "Twisted Sister" and "Brain Damage"—with a smaller "Pink Floyd" name below it. I was married, with two kids owned a home and had been an undercover narcotics cop for seven of the last eight years. Hadn't worn a uniform in five years.

Now, I was full-fledged police detective.

Suit. White shirt. Tie. Short hair.

To quote legendary author Raymond Chandler from his famous crime mystery novel *The Big Sleep*: "I was neat, clean, shaved and sober, and I didn't care who knew it."

Except for one thing: I did care. I'd expected to remain in the Vice Squad, working in the narcotics division, doing what I'd been trained to do, even if it was off-beat and meant taking a lot of risks.

But on a Friday afternoon I was promoted and on the following Sunday afternoon I was neat, clean, shaved...

My wife at the time loved seeing me all cleaned up and nicely dressed. My kids were too little to notice. I was bummed.

Being on the introductory routine detective assignment, with an older detective assigned to break me in for a day, felt as though I were working for nothing. I mean the old "He who sits and serves is as important as those on the front line..." and all that crap, if I even quoted it correctly, is true and I was just doing my job.

But I was bored. The work was mundane and easy, given what I'd recently been doing on the job. I was twenty-nine years old; youthful energy was still my friend.

That did not last long.

I was quickly assigned to one of the busiest detective squads in the city, on the 4:00 p.m. to midnight shift. Major crimes division. A place with rot-gut booze and warm beer chasers—in a manner of speaking.

My partners and I investigated everything from automobile theft rings to homicides, during various parts of the next twenty-two years I was a cop.

And I'd quickly learned that getting away from the narcotics division was the best thing that could have happened. As one might guess, there is a long, long story about my life during those years.

Police officers—even detectives—on routine patrol have their so-called down time. Nothing is happening. You can, and are expected to, make things happen, such as observing and making traffic stops. Keep an eye out for suspicious characters and activities, the great majority of which turns out to be of no consequence. In smaller cities and outlying precincts in larger cities, that's pretty much what police work is all about.

In the high crime, high violence neighborhoods, patrol officers and detectives get ambushed constantly with extremely critical work. Major thefts are to be investigated as soon as possible, and the suspects and, hopefully, the property to be tracked down. Then burglaries. Up from there to robberies. That's where things get intense and all stops are pulled from their heretofore comfortable places in the machine. Experienced, hardworking detectives—sometimes politics inserts the undeserving—work on those assignments.

I got to the more important investigations soon enough. Spent time in court during the day, investigating heinous criminal activities at night. Attended the occasional autopsy of a murder victim, whatever time the medical examiner wanted.

As all of us in this position do, I got to know lots of people, fellow police officers, businessmen and women, attorneys (loves me my lawyers!) and criminals. Lots and lots of criminals. It is from that group that cops endure the heavy, life-changing attitudes. Which leads some officers to alcoholism, the most well-known difficulty to which cops succumb. There's more, darker stuff that some cops get into.

But you're a hero, a star, and if you want, you can play it up with any number of easily impressed and downright naive audiences.

My partner and I would see a lot of cops at the headquarters building downtown at the beginning of our shift. There were always men and women from precincts in the Detective Bureau assembly processing their cases. All of the normal, expected human interactions of those meetings and greetings were exchanged every day.

"Hi, guys," we'd say to others and they'd all say it back. Maybe some small talk. Then hit the bricks.

There's one thing you can't do, and there's one supreme police experience underscoring the certain cop attitude that is often on display from police officers.

One night at about ten o'clock your squad radio suddenly blasts an agonized voice shouting, "We need help!" And then you hear nothing. Seconds go by. You sense the entire force of officers on the street monitoring their police radios, in frozen, agonizing positions.

And waiting. A half a minute goes by. Then, you hear—

"—Officer down!"

That only means one thing.

The radio goes quiet once again. It is a time of insanity as you're forced to wait some more. A highly stressed, almost nonhuman voice eventually shouts out a location over the radio. Every available squad heads there, double time.

Some officers are only a couple blocks away. When that's the case—as it was with me—you come upon the scene only moments after the event occurred. We arrived. It was a long abandoned pool hall in the worst part of the city. Police squad cars and their red lights flashing arrive and park willy-nilly. One on the side walk next to the building. An ambulance joins the crowd. Inside the pool hall is an obviously homeless type guy, laying on his back. Paramedics pushing on his chest, fixing an oxygen mask to his face.

Another plainclothes officer, his face spattered with blood, stands a few paces back. He has fixed his half-hooded eyes at the paramedics and the obviously dead man who shot his partner.

The wounded officer has already been conveyed to an ambulance.

A couple other officers in the place—blanched faces, wide eyes, guns drawn. You look back through a window at an ambulance parked outside with paramedics inside pressing on the chest of a fine officer, dressed in plain clothes, as he lay motionless on a gurney. The paramedics press. And they press, and they press...

You remember saying "Hi" to both officers earlier in the shift; somewhere on the street, or in a precinct. You'll never remember exactly where.

They take the dead, homeless looking dude who'd shot him point-blank in the chest to another ambulance that arrived at the scene in the street.

Other officers arrive and help work the scene inside the dark, dingy old pool hall.

After a short while, a lieutenant quietly announces, "He didn't make it."

Everyone keeps working soundlessly, as though they hadn't heard him speak the words. Everyone is a professional. Everyone handles their assignments properly. It is quiet. You could hear a pin drop. A couple of hours later you're finished and you head downtown.

The blood and the spent shell casings and the chalk marks outlining where the bodies had been and one chalk mark circling a hole in the wall of an errant bullet, mash together in your mind while you fill out your reports. You feel it. Your disbelieving mind. But then you don't feel anything. And no one says anything. But you feel something build anyway: a hard, dense sensation starting as a small point in the center of your chest, steadily growing larger and stronger. And you know it will never leave.

On your way home from work you stop at a nightclub owned by your good friend and tell him a cop was murdered. He's staring at your face.

"You investigate it?" he asks.

You answer in the affirmative and he gives you a large, full glass of rot-gut booze. Forget the chaser.

You have another glass of booze. It wasn't until later, when I was drunk enough to let go that I realized...
...I was devastated.

# SEVEN
*Lacy*

The Detective Captain standing at the podium was not well-liked. Most days we'd see him in the Detective Bureau assembly at about 3:45 p.m., tall, slim, hard bodied. He had a big nose and wore thick-rimmed glasses. He was openly taunted and even mocked by older detectives who'd been partners with him before he was promoted. He was there each day to give roll call, which meant that he'd read descriptions of suspects for serious crimes committed during the previous twenty-four hours.

This time, he surprised us by saying loudly: "Regarding that prisoner who died in our custody last night, the matter's been resolved. There was no wrong-doing on our part." He then began reading roll call, as usual.

I looked at the detectives sitting near me and they all returned my glance. *What the hell is he talking about?* was stamped on all of our faces. We shrugged and began listening to the descriptions.

Afterward, we were all quick to learn that none of us had heard anything about the prisoner who'd "died in our custody" the night before.

"What's up, Captain?" someone called out.

He picked up some papers from the podium and began walking toward his office. "No time to explain. The Early Shift bosses will fill you in."

We all returned to our own business, dismissing what the captain had said. We were sure to never think of it again.

But the remark involved an incident that kicked off a nationwide, headline grabbing news story. A story that would have a major impact on the police use of force on everyone they arrested, from the time people were first in custody until the time they were released by the courts. The impact would extend to every police department across the country, *From New York City to Los Angel-ees*, as the old time radio hype-sters would have put it.

It was the story of the arrest of one Ernest Lacy for a crime he did not commit.

Now, the arresting officers had probable cause to stop and frisk Mr. Lacy, based on the just-broadcast description of a rape suspect. In their minds he fit the description of the suspect. Ordinarily he would have been checked out, as they say, and released after a short time.

No problem there.

But Mr. Lacy resisted the officers when they explained why they'd stopped him. Not at all uncommon, that a man would pull away from policemen who told him he was being investigated for a rape. What innocent man wouldn't feel panic, believing he was about to be charged with a heinous crime that he did not commit? What innocent man's body under such circumstances wouldn't compulsively seize up, his breath and heartbeat launching to light speed? And on and on.

But the officers claimed that Ernest Lacy fought with them. As hard as he possibly could and tried to escape their custody. The officers insisted they'd only held him with strong force as long as was necessary.

A police conveyance wagon was called to the scene.

While waiting, the officers handcuffed Mr. Lacy behind his back and placed on him on the ground, on his stomach, to keep him restrained. All normal procedures. A young woman watched from across the street and said it seemed to her that Lacy had surrendered. Some would strongly suspect the officers continued their pressure longer than was necessary. But the law stated officers were allowed to use as much force as was reasonable and necessary.

Everything boiled down to that point in the arrest: had Mr. Lacy given up, or blacked out, before the officers let him up from the ground? How would—or could—anyone determine what his condition had been after the fact?

Mr. Lacy was found to be unconscious and unresponsive after the prisoner wagon arrived at the precinct. He was rushed to the hospital where he was pronounced dead.

Later that evening and the next day, representatives of the Milwaukee Chief of Police and the Milwaukee County District Attorney convened. The initial opinion announced—no one ever did admit making that initial official announcement—was the officers used reasonable force.

All of the district and department commanders told officers reporting for duty the following day that everything about the Ernie Lacy case was good. Ha ha ha.

A local defense attorney—later made famous as the attorney representing a woman charged with murder, played by the late Farrah Fawcett in the made-for-TV movie *The Burning Bed*—was hired by Mr. Lacy's surviving relatives.

Every law officer and official in southeastern Wisconsin knew it was only the beginning of the matter. They knew it before Mr. Eisenberg even began his investigation, because he had a well-documented reputation for believing the Milwaukee Police Department was rife with brutal officers and he would approach this matter with a standard accusation that the police had over reacted while making the arrest. Since Lacy was African American, the case took on strong racial overtones. Officers and other officials expected Attorney Eisenberg to reject any finding or opinion that the officers had acted properly.

He did.

It was expected he would suggest to the local news media that the officers had used too much force while subduing Mr. Lacy.

Which he did.

Three subsequent autopsies found Lacy's cause of death to be undetermined.

Other than saying the officers had done nothing wrong, Chief Breier remained silent. Large groups of people, from across the nation with high-profile reputations for their involvement with such events, gathered and marched in the streets. The national news media monitored the situation and made regular reports. Editorials appeared in most newspapers, coast to coast. The officers believed they were being tried in the press, as it were, without all the facts being presented to the citizenry. The prevailing opinion was the officers had acted improperly—that they had, indeed, murdered Ernest Lacy.

Ultimately the best guess was Lacy had died from asphyxiation, when an officer knelt on his back as he lay face down. There had never been another case of this kind, where death resulted from the technique of police officers placing of a person on their stomach while subduing them.

After nearly a full month of testimony and more than one hundred witnesses being called, an inquest recommended the officers be charged with reckless homicide and misconduct in office.

District Attorney E. Michael McCann charged the officers with the recommended crimes. The case was later dismissed at the preliminary hearing due to a lack of evidence to proceed to a trial. Word from highly respected sources was that no assistant district attorney had been willing to try the case without being ordered to do so. With three autopsies finding no discernible cause of death, how could you proceed with criminal charges? It was by then a highly charged political matter with many powerful public officials stating their belief that the officers had committed a crime.

Shocked police training officials throughout the nation said they could see no alternative to pinning the man to the ground, that it was a matter of individual judgment as to when, or if, he'd stopped resisting, and that less force could then be used while restraining him. How could an officer know where to draw the line, when the person was possibly getting the better of the encounter?

The Fire and Police Commission was off the hook of making their own decision about disciplining the officers; the recommended charges by the inquest sufficiently backed them up when they fired one officer and imposed lengthy unpaid suspensions on three others.

It took almost two years to reach the end of the matter. Pathologists were taken off guard when no cause of death could be found. A new term was coined: Positional Asphyxiation, meaning if a person lays too long on their stomach, with too much pressure on their back, they can suffocate. It can't necessarily be proven, but it is obviously a dangerous technique. From then on, officers needed to have prisoners in a seated position if it were deemed necessary to place them on the ground.

Many vicious and provably untrue accusations were made against the police along the way. This was standard procedure by certain people who always protested when a citizen was injured during an arrest. I knew this for a fact because I was a member of the department; an officer with more than ten years' experience, I understood what had happened. People with no experience, and who had been deliberately misinformed because of that fact, accepted the claims without knowing the truth. The moment that most affected me was, after the judge dismissed the case, a local TV camera was pointed at Ernest Lacy's mother, who then claimed the D.A. told her afterward the officers "were guilty of murdering Ernest."

There was never a meaningful public discussion of that remark. We on the police department tried to keep tabs on it, to see if it was ever addressed—by the news media, or by the District Attorney's office. None was ever noted.

In the minds of millions of Americans, the officers were guilty. Even though there was never a trial, much less an official finding of guilt.

# EIGHT
### Santa Claus

Christmas time has always meant more action on the family-trouble home-front. Of course, it doesn't end there; the anticipation of happiness and celebration during the season can provoke the unhappiness, and downright depression, of those who have problems in their lives. Calls for police intervention in domestic disturbances, and trouble elsewhere, have always seen an increase—both in the number of calls and the strangeness of calls. The word about this specific time for fights among family members has been known about by society at large for many generations.

The usual suspect of increased motivation for bad behavior has been the extra imbibing of alcohol because of more partying and increased drinking of said booze. Like stocking up the home for the extra visiting that will happen and then the sampling of the extra stock of booze during the weeks leading up to the Big Day, December 25th. Which means more people being overly drunk, more often than usual.

And, of course, the nightclubs and neighborhood taverns make more money during this particular holiday season—with all the pre-Christmas imbibing by customers as they stop in for the parties. Or after they've spent the day and/or night shopping for gifts.

I could analyze it deeper—so-called social scientists have done quite enough of that—but everyone knows that along with the increase in happiness and celebrations, there is also an increase in trouble on the home-front.

The booze drinking and the attendant tension increases for about a month preceding Christmas Day multiplies from Thanksgiving Day. Every now and then, there is a combination of Christmas trouble from both the families and other places in the streets. Ultimately, the behavior of the perpetrators of Christmas time trouble is nothing more than drunken, stupid nonsense. Sometimes the drunken nonsense gets violent. It can be dangerous and in the worst cases, deadly. And when the clashes occur between crazy drunk strangers, it takes on a somehow different, often bizarre quality.

One Christmas season about fifty years ago there was a legendary Christmas crisis on the south side of Milwaukee. That area of the world was generally pretty tame, pretty quiet, a good place to raise children and get them reasonably well-educated. And a good place to stay safe from crime and violence. One Christmas Eve broke all imaginable boundaries the of normal heated, drunken condition.

The Dark Side of Christmas, if you will.

A family-trouble fight and a shopping store, uh, how shall we say, "disturbance," came together. A group of officers were blessed with the task of handling the situation. And as the old saying goes, *it wasn't pretty.*

First off, stores closed early on Christmas Eve in those days. Some of the larger ones in more heavily populated areas stayed open late: until eight o'clock! And one of those stores on a south side main street and shopping area was one of those places. In the doorway leading into the store stood a man wearing a—ta da!—Santa Claus suit. He was ringing a hand-held bell loudly and shouting "Ho, ho, ho!" to all who passed by and/or entered the store. He cheerfully encouraged passersby to place money into the nearby bucket. Many passersby did, and some did not.

Now, the Santa Claus knew he'd be outdoors for hours. But he was smart. He knew his extra-heavy Santa Claus clothing would not be enough to keep him warm. So he rigged up a rubber tube connected to a bottle of whiskey in his pocket and merrily sucked on the end of the tube, which he'd cleverly hidden in his big, fake white beard.

Guess what?

He got drunk.

Slowly at first, when he was jolly and fun-loving and a classic hail-fellows-well-met character. Ringing his big bell, collecting money, joking with the folks. But then he decided that not enough folks were putting enough money into the bucket. Who wouldn't be annoyed about that during the ultimate, charitable time of year, right?

But the more whiskey he sucked through his rubber tube, the less jolly he became. He became irritable with folks who didn't give money.

"Too cheap to help the needy?" he said to one man and his family who failed to contribute anything.

They were shocked and proceeded into the store to make a complaint.

Sarcastic remarks followed every non-contributor. Quietly spoken at first, then loud sarcastic remarks. Really loud and really insulting ones. Oh, it didn't last too long. Before the store management could react, another man who'd been cruisin' and boozin' on the streets confronted Mr. Santa Claus. Name calling began. Fists flew. The police were called. Santa Claus was hauled off kicking and screaming to a prisoner conveyance wagon.

The other guy went to jail, too.

Santa and the other guy were hauled to the 6th Precinct and placed in holding cells. They could hear each other, so they continued screaming and yelling mindless insults. Officers on desk duty at the station house separated them to different rooms, leaving Santa in the cell block.

A couple of miles away a Christmas party began after dinner in a residence packed with visitors. Young children were there. Many adults were there. Lots and lots of booze, in every mixed and swirled way you can think of, was there. Came time to open presents. Grandpa dressed as Santa Claus sat in front of the brightly lighted Christmas tree. The classic scene. Later, after everything was over, a woman said he'd been smoked full of liquor and "you know what" other stuff.

That's right—"other stuff" was available and used fifty years ago, before the so-called hippie out-break of the 1960s

One by one the kids came up to sit on his lap. He instantly got fed up with it. He started calling the kids little brats who deserved spankings, not presents. The little brats' parents didn't take it so well. One of the fathers—who had also been smoked to the high heavens with inebriates—approached the surprisingly spry Santa and pushed him off his chair. A fight among those two and a few others in the room broke out. The tree was toppled and the lights were smashed.

The police were called and while being arrested Santa Claus delivered a groin disintegrating kick to one of the officers. He fought and he fought and he fought. He visited the 6th Precinct station.

The officers who dragged him in to the building took him straight to the holding cell. Normal procedure. But on this occasion: different. The first drunken Santa Claus sitting in his cell saw the second drunken Santa Claus being dragged past. The first Santa still had enough energy left to jump up and spit a large amount of phlegm onto the second Santa Claus. Onto the officers, too.

The second Santa Claus managed to slip the grasp of

the officers who were holding him and charged toward the closed and locked—thank the heavens!—cell door, grabbed the bars and smashed his own forehead against them. That's right, his own forehead. The Santa inside the cell grabbed the bars from his side and attempted to smash his head into that of the first Santa.

They called each other names like "phony" and "faker" and worse. They both declared how each had made a better Santa Claus than the other. Well, more than one police officer on the scene said that's what happened, and I believe it's absolutely true. At least the stupid, ear-splitting screaming that went on. No one could deny the screaming.

Other officers in the precinct, including the shift commander, came into the cell block to help the arresting officer remove the second drunker-than-a-skunk Santa they had brought in. They wanted to separate them, but more prisoners had been brought in during the meantime and all other make-shift rooms were rapidly being filled. For a short while both Santas were held in the same cell block room, while adjustments to the station house were being made.

It was not a Merry Christmas.

Soon, both of the hyper-but-stinking-screaming-drunk Santas began to run out of gas. Literally, as the room had quickly become in drastic need of deodorizing. But that's what always goes on in relatively small rooms filled with screaming drunks. In a short while, the Santas, and a few other drunks who'd been hauled in and joined the laughter and name-calling, grew quiet.

Both of the exhausted, mind obliterated Santas lay down on their benches behind the bars, closed their eyes, and went fast asleep.

Parts of that tale from the blue line may seem unbelievable. Trust me. After thirty years of being in the middle of my share of equally crazy scenes, I know it happened, very closely to the way it was told. Too many cops were there and they all had similar stories. And there's a long blue column of people with police experience, past and present, who will silently nod their heads, with thoughtful expressions on their faces, and maybe a slight smile, and know this was just another day in the park, as it were, for these poor Christmas coppers on that Christmas Eve in Milwaukee, fifty years ago.

# NINE
## Occupy Wall Street

Social get-togethers in the streets to protest things—
Occupy Wall Street, for example—are as old as time
itself. People deign to take time from the important
business of living life in order to point out and focus on
what they feel is bad behavior by some who have gained
power in our society. They also accomplish a whole lot
of stuff which could be called under the radar. Some of
the stuff is also against the law. A common side business
is selling illegal drugs. How do I know? Because I used
to attend similar roundups years ago. Oh, I wasn't
protesting or advocating for anyone or anything: I was
an undercover narcotics cop who was assigned to check
things out for—gasp!—the government.

Occupy Wall Street borrowed from a tried and not-
so-true protest style that was made bigger than ever—
not necessarily in size or effectiveness, but rather in
public attention and notoriety—back in the days when
astute protestors were protesting the protest du jour: the
Vietnam War. What a time that was. What a big bunch
of protests they flung. And my assignment—which was
only on a few occasions, thank goodness—was to
infiltrate and gather intelligence from the protest leaders
and the mobs of young people who followed them.

I've used some pejoratives to describe the protests
and their leaders and followers. I am truly sorry. I wish
things had been different.

By the time I did my assignments—from 1971 to
1973—undercover work had been well established in

covering the protest movements of the era. Some young officers across the country did deep undercover assignments, where they actually attended university classes and lived in apartments on or near the campuses. Officers learned anti-government plans fostered by people—some students, but the leaders were much older—who were at absolutely total ideological odds with the majority of those in elected offices at the time.

Some have come back into view in recent years, as anyone who follows the news is aware.

The deep undercovers got the truly important information, which turned out to be nothing. The FBI got the main stuff, which was what really counted. I talked to more than one of the city undercover people after they returned to regular duty—they became detectives, one was a sergeant—and they all said it was largely a waste of time.

There was a core group of people with strong, and strongly expressed, opinions about the war in Vietnam and Presidents Johnson—is this old news rubble or what?!—and Nixon. As far as the real threat, the threat of terrorist violence or real possibilities of a violent, revolutionary takeover of the United States of America, it was a laugh. But it had to be checked and the powers that be in law enforcement figured out the level of threat that these people proposed to the country: the lowest.

I'm speaking of the young-uns and handful of whacky oldsters who gathered at government buildings and the like. All they did was make noise. I know that is true. I saw it. The less-than-a-handful of damaged sites and dead bodies they produced—an era which quickly ended—had been overrated and over feared. That's what I heard from other officers, and again, that is what I saw.

But there was some fun to be had by the pre-OWS protestors: Drugs! And Sex! And Drugs! And Sex! By the time I was taking on those assignments—which were only a few by the early 1970s—that was virtually the only reason most of the people attended the protests. Finding one-night-stands for sexual relief and dope was the thing. Many of the drug using college students relied heavily on the marches and protests to make friends with drug suppliers. Many drug suppliers grew their hair long and wore beards and so-called hippie clothing of the day, just to mingle with the buyers at the protest sites. And make money. For a while, lotsa money.

Mostly people sat around waiting for their deliveries and did all manner of trash talk. About all manner of subjects. They'd drink alcohol and smoke pot all day and crash at the sites that were open 24/7. I, personally, was bored out of my mind, keeping an eye out for drugsters, an ear open for big talk from faux revolutionaries about how they were gonna rip this place apart—meaning the U.S. of A.—and somehow make it into to that utopian place the wise elders had talked up in previous centuries. Or something like that.

One time some college students and their street associates set up a political discussion in a large basement room used for that kind of thing in one of the larger campus buildings. The university shall remain unnamed, but it did have some of the best college basketball programs in the country at the time and even won an NCAA basketball tournament a couple of generations ago.

The inside word was that revolutionaries and overall anarchic leaders were going to perform street theater and teach the attendees about how life should truly be organized and lived by the people. The police department caught word and sent my partner and I to take notes. Actually, we were there to make drug connections because that was the only true law breaking that might be going on.

As the theater began, several young men wearing field jackets and hats ran into the room, making zooming sounds like airplanes and throwing small paper airplanes at the people sitting there. A paper airplane hit me in the face. I laughed. A young man told me dead people don't laugh: I had just been a victim of a bomb dropping airplane. He then said it takes time to learn street theater, so he understood my inappropriate reaction.

Others from his group each took a turn shouting out a single anti-war sentence. Then the person next to him, and so on. It was very dramatic. Shortly thereafter everyone stood and began mingling, talking about the war and the unfairness of the system. Some started to leave. A line formed in back at a table where a couple of guys were surreptitiously swapping marijuana joints and nickel bags for money. My partner and I quickly got in line but they had sold out before we got there.

Oh, and the protest gathering was summarily dismissed in a loud, officious voice by one of the paper airplane bomber people. He said one day it would be real—that Americans would be killed by our enemies everywhere, even in our own country.

At least one thing said that night was the truth.

The upper command officers of the police department demanded undercover officers continue monitoring the rapidly shrinking gatherings. Our bosses told us to go there and if things shaped up the same every time, where absolutely nothing criminal was going on, we could leave. And that's what happened until we were never assigned to a social or war protest again.

In truth, college protesting on campuses—or anywhere else, for that matter—took a major hit when the four students at Kent State University were shot and killed by the National Guard on May 4th, 1970.

I was long retired when the Occupy Wall Street

crowds began to gather in September of 2011, first in Manhattan, and then, well...Manhattan was the only real one. A few others elsewhere were known about because of the news media, but they never made much noise. I made friendly bets with some neighbors that OWS would fizzle out. They were shameless sucker bets, as it quickly became apparent. At least I didn't take their money.

But there was new twist to the coverage: news people swamped the areas and were shocked at how ridiculous many of the protestors were—*and they actually told the world the real story*. The news people watched protestors openly scavenge for drugs and use them on the spot. Of course, how some also scavenged for sex, only nowadays they did it on the spot. Usually after dark. OWS had more interlopers committing crimes—primarily rape and theft.

No one gave cogent, informed answers about the issues they were protesting. That's exactly how it was forty years earlier when I wasted my time, er, when I swept through throngs of scary people who were plotting the end of the world as we know it.

# TEN
## *Teacher*

Abraham Lincoln was, by all accounts, a genius. He specialized in the law and was considered to be brilliant. He understood the law and how it needed to operate and be enforced. He was also the sixteenth president of the United States. But he made his bones, as they say these days, through his experiences as a lawyer.

That said, many places of glory in America have been named after him, from The Land of Lincoln—Illinois—to streets and bridges in virtually every municipality. Among the sacred places named for him are schools. There is one high school in Milwaukee named Lincoln High School. It was built in the 1930s in one of Milwaukee's elite neighborhoods. The kids there were smart, hardworking, good athletes. Many received scholarships to universities.

In the late 1950s and early 1960s Lincoln High School produced some of the finest basketball teams the state has ever seen. They won state championship after state championship. By then the neighborhood had blended with African American families. Every one of the state championship teams was comprised of young African American players. They were brilliant athletes and excellent students. Most received scholarships and played at major universities. A few of them went on to play in the National Basketball Association. One went on to be a federal court judge. But as time swiftly moved on, the neighborhood had deteriorated, and a gradual lessening of both academic and behavioral standards began to take over. It was a classic abandonment of housing and business structures as they grew old. The 1960s came and the influx of drugs that exploded during the decade was quick and massive. Everyone everywhere was affected. Part of the youth scene had become a veritable burning bush of marijuana cigarettes, pipes, bongs and anything else that was usable.

Police departments in major cities were inundated with illegal drug investigations. Drugs were being sold everywhere, on the streets, in the bars and, tragically, in the schools. No one knew how to deal with it. It was all learn-by-doing for the cops, especially young cops, because of the youth of the users and dealers. Young guys could look like and pretend they were dopers. They could—and did—make lots of drug arrests.

In Milwaukee the neighborhoods surrounding the high schools were mobbed with teenagers walking around during their lunch period, cutting through yards and alleys and smoking dope. At any given high school during lunch, there often were as many as one hundred such students involved in this activity. It was madness for the school officials who had classrooms filled with students high at least on marijuana, for the citizens whose properties were being polluted with substance polluted youngsters, and of course, for the police departments with districts containing high schools.

In 1974 things were as bad as they would ever be. I was one of four young Milwaukee cops assigned to the undercover section of the narcotics squad, dressed in ragged street clothes, and drove out in our private vehicles to school after school after school. We quickly learned to hate it. We were badly outnumbered and forced to police the outer sections of the lunchtime dopers. We'd arrest kids with dope—small amounts— place them in the back seats of our own cars, and drive off. We quickly became known at every school and had to change cars and get-ups in order to avoid being attacked. We were attacked a lot anyway and made plenty of arrests on that basis.

One can imagine what a pain in the ass that duty was.

But we hung in there and received the admiration and accolades of our commanding officers.

This brings me back to Lincoln High School—a place named for perhaps the greatest American in history.

One day we young, School Patrol officers were divided up into two private automobiles. It was Lincoln High School's turn to be surrounded and lose a few students from the classrooms to the nearest juvenile holding cell. And for said students to lose their stash of dope.

We got there just before lunchtime on a sunny, mild autumn day. We chatted with each other a bit on the handie-talkie radios, as they used to be called, and set up to watch the school's doors. The bell rang. Always a sickening sound, we knew the ill-behaved ones were soon to explode out of all exits. As usual, it wasn't long before we saw a small group of teenage boys huddle together in an alley a block away, light up and pass a marijuana smoking bowl. A pot pipe, for the experts who don't like the unhip, official description of the smoking device.

"Smoke a bowl and lose control," I remember saying to myself. I remember it because it was my personal ritual to at least think the words every time I watched a gathering of ne'er do wells begin their illegal indulgence.

The four of us narcs watched with binoculars and when we were satisfied they'd all smoked from the bowl, we drove up to the youngsters from both directions to where they stood in the alley. Of course, we observed the odor of marijuana and had probable cause to search the group. Ninety-five percent of the time the kids were so flummoxed they froze in place and gave up. We confiscated the dope, and the kids, and took them to HQ. Headquarters, which I'm sure you all knew, but we shortened it up while communicating on the street. Sometimes they struggled a bit, often times they started crying and begging to be let go. Sometimes they said, "Fuck you, pig!" and ran.

Guess what happened this time?

They ran. The four of us did the thing we hated most—we ran after them. The leader of their pack ran to the school and entered. We were surprised. His compadres followed. Huh. They were trapping themselves. Oh, well. Teenage dopers weren't all that hardened.

Thus, the real fun began. The boys were gone from our sight by the time we got into the school. I personally couldn't identify even one of them. I followed my partner who could. We checked the boys' rooms. Nothing. We checked closets and anything that might look like a hiding place. Nothing. A janitor—who I suspected of being on the booze a bit—told us students weren't allowed to run around in school. We looked at each other and laughed. We looked at the—I'm certain—drunken janitor, shook our heads, and kept running around the school. We saw no students.

The bell rang again and those who'd left the school poured back in. One young girl walked toward us, stopped, and pointed to a classroom. She turned her head and walked away. We waited until things settled in the classroom and slowly entered. I had no idea who we were looking for. But one of my partners did. He looked in the back and saw one teenager slumped in a chair.

Bingo!

One problem. The teacher watched us with a burning stare and fiercely folded arms. She was African American, about five feet tall, middle aged.

"Who are you?" she shouted.

I flinched. The trouble we were facing with, hopefully, making an arrest, assuaging school officials, calling for a conveyance wagon, and writing lengthy detailed reports, was all I could think of.

"You!" my partner said, pointing at the boy.

We all showed our badges to the teacher and one of us began talking to HQ on the handie-talkie. She accepted our identification without question. She looked at the boy my partner was pointing to, pointed to us, and said, "These are Milwaukee police officers! Freeze!"

The diminutive teacher literally pushed past us and approached the boy. "Keep your hands where I can see them!"

We stood near to the blackboard at the front of the classroom and began to follow her.

"You are under arrest!" she shouted.

By this time she'd reached him in his chair. "Get up!" she said.

The boy quickly and quietly stood. The teacher waved to us while staring at the hapless student. When we got to her she clasped her arms together and stepped back.

"What did he do?" she asked.

We told her.

"Well, then, cuff him and take him outta here!" she yelled.

I fumbled for my handcuffs and placed them on the child. The four of us narcs silently looked at the teacher.

"One of you come with me to the office and explain what he did," she said, as we all walked out the door.

Three of us walked with the handcuffed youngster to the exit. We were all speechless. Stunned is a more accurate word. Being the senior officer, I followed the teacher to the office. She explained everything to the principal, interrupting herself at times to ask me questions about the arrest.

"Good job," she said to me while I was leaving. "I'll call Mayor Maier first chance I get."

I quietly left the school and joined up with my partners and our prisoner. He eventually told us who his accomplices were.

To this day I scratch my head when I think about who really made that drug arrest at Lincoln High School, back in 1974.

# ELEVEN
## *Grandpa*

Heavy raindrops beat the roof of the unmarked squad car I was riding in like a tom-tom. I didn't like it. No one did. We detectives would see each other on the street or at various precincts and stop to whine about it. As one could figure, those nights were slow for cops; everyone stayed inside. Of course, this didn't happen on every chilly, rainy springtime night. Some of those nights were notoriously busy.

One of those nights was a nightmare for every human being who was forced to be at a particular crime scene in one of thousands of neighborhood blocks in the city.

A dispatch came over the main police radio—the high ban, they called it—where all squads assigned to a given area could hear the call. Some chatter about family-trouble at an address somewhere and then the continued droning of the conversing officers. My partner and I were miles away and paid it no mind.

A short while later a Detective Lieutenant spoke on the second radio we carried—the portable handie-talkie—from the headquarters desk to a detective squad patrolling the area of the family-trouble call. He spoke in a clipped, serious tone, wanting to know how long it would take the detectives to arrive at the scene.

My partner and I perked up, looked at the radio where it sat on the dashboard and then looked at each other. The lieutenant who was speaking was a top guy, a supervisor they'd look for to handle the serious, important cases. The radio quickly went quiet. The high ban radio that dispatched uniform squads to its calls was also quiet. The tom-tom rainfall pounded the roof of the car, as though it were a drummer at a Dave Clark Five rock concert.

Something was wrong—very wrong—at the family-trouble address. However, things were always going wrong in this city. We didn't get the assignment, so we got on with our lives.

And then we did get the assignment. It was not in our assigned district—a clue that something major had happened. The shift commander had taken the lieutenant's place at the office desk, a sign the lieutenant was on his way to supervise the crime scene. But aside from the drumming of the rain, it was quiet.

I always sensed a grim crime scene under those conditions.

We drove to the family-trouble scene and parked a half block away. Both marked and unmarked squads had been sent before us; a couple of them were parked askew in the street. Also askew to the curb was an old, dirty and seriously dented up white van. It had no side windows. A barrier of the classic yellow police tape ringed the van, protecting it from the unauthorized. A lone uniformed officer, wearing his full complement of rain gear, stood next to it. He stood at semi-attention...quiet...serious...reflective looking. It added to the ominous atmosphere.

My partner and I approached the van. It was empty, but the dome light was on. I nodded at the officer as we walked past and he rolled his eyes. My partner and I exchanged glances. We were in for it.

The house we'd been sent to was completely lit up. Shades were pulled up. I could see the thick raindrops falling straight down through the glare. I could hear them steadily drumming on the rooftops of the nearby houses. Aside from that it was eerily quiet. The screaming and yelling that usually accompanies family fighting was not to be heard.

We entered the home through the side door. The house was packed with people, both citizens and officers. The lieutenant saw us and worked his way through the group to where we were. He began explaining our assignment.

A despised grandfather—smashed to the gills and beyond by booze—had shown up to, ah, visit. Everyone who lived there hated him...more specifically—they didn't want to see or be with him in any way. An extremely common family scenario in the neighborhood we were in. Everyone had dutifully cleared out of his way while one of them went to get him food.

The lieutenant stopped and said the police photographer had just gone out to the van. "Riley, you go with him. There's a copper out there who can guide you guys through."

I left, unprepared for what I was going to experience—how could I have been? I rounded the back corner of the house and approached the street in front. A uniformed officer assigned to the Traffic Division was taking photographs—standard MPD procedure.

"What's up?" I asked when I arrived at the van.

The traffic officer let his camera hang by the strap around his neck and looked at me—a forced, strange look... one intended to notify me that what was up was not good.

"Take a look in the van," he said pointing to the small windows on the vehicle doors.

I knew there'd be a bad scene: a body, some kind of unimaginable mess.

I was right.

The body of a dead girl—eight years old I would later learn—lay on her back. The girl had been wearing a light colored dress, which was lifted up...covering her face and exposing her nude bottom half.

Blood...a thick smear where the legs joined the torso and a dark, gaping channel in the center.

I became aware of my head twisting slightly from side to side. It had started on its own...involuntarily shaking. My lips parted, my jaw dropped. All the clichés describing a person who is, not just in shock or stupefied, not simply horrified, but frozen in a way that would leave you forever changed.

"Some grandpas 'love' their grandchildren more than others, I guess," the officer taking photos said sarcastically.

I realized he'd been watching me for who-knew-how-long.

I looked at him and saw the same expression on his face I knew was still on mine. The bullshit joke had come from the lips, but the energy, the upbeat twinkle normally registering in the eyes of the joke maker was not there.

His gaze grew quizzical. "You know what happened, don't you?"

I was embarrassed. I was a detective, one of the officers in charge of the scene, but things had been happening so fast, and in such a staccato motion, the detail of how this child had come to her end had not been explicitly stated to me.

The officer's shoulders sagged, his eyelids dropped. He was going to have to tell me the details of a murder.

"Grandpa came over drunk out of his mind. A fight broke out. He said he wanted to play with his granddaughter. He grabbed her by the arm and took her to the van here." He pointed at the vehicle. "Her mother wasn't here and the two young boys in the living room were afraid to follow."

"'Grandpa did this?" I said.

"Yeah. The kids checked on the van about a half

hour later. He was lying on top of her. Passed out. She wasn't moving."

One of the boys had called 9-1-1 and the first responding officers dragged the old dude off of her.

The rest of the routine part of the investigation moved along: Grandpa was taken to jail, the paramedics arrived and declared the child dead, the medical examiner was en route, more police officers arrived, interviews were begun.

It was obvious the girl had been raped and then strangled or suffocated by the drunken weight of a man who should have been protecting her...not...this.

After a long pause I looked at the officer and said, "A head's up would have been nice."

"We're all in shock," he snapped defensively.

And he was right. When you're unexpectedly thrown into a wicked, deranged scene that should never, ever be allowed to even exist, you get kind of loopy.

The police photographer and I were both kind of loopy.

I mechanically brought out my memorandum book and began writing notes. The sound of people screeching emanated from the back of the house. A moment later the lieutenant called and waved to me to join him on the front sidewalk.

"I gotta go call the boss," he said while I approached. "The girl's mother just came home, with her sister. She doesn't know the whole story. You think they were screaming before. Just wait..."

He stopped speaking. I was ready to keep listening, but the silence stretched out. After a moment he said, "Everyone else is busy. You gotta do the notification."

He looked down and away and walked toward his squad car.

I went into the back of the house and was ushered into the kitchen. Only the stove light was on. The girl's mother was sitting at the kitchen table, sobbing. Everyone else walked out as I entered, brushing past me.

I was about to enact the most despised ritual there is for a cop.

I looked at the woman, whose head was rapidly turning from side to side. Why is everyone leaving? One could almost hear her think.

Her eyes rested on me for the answer.

"Is my baby going to be okay?" she asked, her voice emitting a heart-wrenching tremolo.

From somewhere deep within I ginned up the answer, but it stuck in my throat like cotton...the image of the poor child forever emblazoned in my mind. I managed to swallow and move it along...

# TWELVE
## *Summerfest*

Some called him Le Roy, others called him Elroy. I called him both names depending upon my mood and state of sobriety. But being called more than one name suited him: Le Roy/Elroy was a multiple kind of guy, who'd go anywhere and do anything

By the way, neither name was his real one.

But we settled on Le Roy and the bosses loved to give him assignments. He didn't wait to get informants, he'd go out and hit on dopers and drug dealers wherever he found them. There were times when we didn't want to know. And he made lots of cases. It was personality, not police work, but it didn't matter. He locked 'em up.

He locked four of them up one time and it made national news. It was one of the most amazing and unbelievable things I ever saw and anyone who has spent significant time as a police officer—especially in a major city like Milwaukee, New York, Chicago or Los Angeles—is a bona fide, certified observer of amazing and unbelievable things. It was a major pain for one of America's top pop singers in the 1970s, but she had to stand back and watch it all unfold.

But I'm getting ahead of myself.

Without a doubt the most dangerous and wild-assed assignment I ever had as a police officer was working undercover on narcotics at Milwaukee's Summerfest celebration, which occurs every summer in July. I'm talking old-days Summerfests, when the festival was first being set up. There was a learning curve with all things and controlling people who'd sneak illegal drugs into the eleven-day-long-party by the shores of Lake Michigan was among the first and largest headaches those in charge ever saw.

It should hereby be noted that I'm writing of a time more than thirty-five years ago. The problem has long since been addressed and resolved. Summerfest is a first class, beautiful and fun festival for the whole family. People come from across the nation to visit Milwaukee during its time each July. The biggest, most well-known bands in the country perform at Summerfest every year and its reputation as a safe, clean place is second to none of its kind anywhere. I personally know this to be a fact.

But the day to which I'm referring was early on. A time when having a hairy, raggedy looking crew of free-spirited and basically fearless people—yes, women were involved also—at their disposal was a heaven send to the people most concerned, from the then-Mayor Henry Maier to then-Police Chief Harold Breier and the entire city council.

It was still light out and festival goers were filing into the grounds, anticipating the performances of a number of rock 'n roll bands, from local groups to nationally known ones, with hit records on their resumes. Our group, facetiously nicknamed "The Rat Patrol," had spent the day in court processing arrests made for using and selling all manner of illegal inebriants the previous day. By early evening we'd checked in with the command post at Summerfest and had begun to walk the grounds to get a feel of the crowd.

As always, we made a few arrests even during the quiet time of the fest, processed them and returned to the grounds. We walked along the shore of Lake Michigan, which was fortified by huge, stone boulders, to protect people from the sometimes fierce waves that could pound the shore. Didn't want the waves pounding on people, of course. In those days the main stage, where all the rock and pop big shots performed, was on the north end of the grounds. The entire area, including the stage itself, the dressing trailers in the back and the long rows of boards upon which the fortunate, and sometimes unfortunate people—a truly long story, sat.

The place was empty as we walked together to the fenced-in area at the back, where the trailers were. Starting time was nigh and the place was filling up with audience members. We saw a couple of uniformed officers, whom we knew at the rear gate, and walked over to say "hi." We chatted amiably: the weather was nice, the band that night was nice—not like some of the hard core street bands, the names of which I shall not write—and everyone was in good spirits.

Except Le Roy. Le Roy trundled off on his own toward the lake shore's edge. The high, sturdy fence stretched to the water line. No one could get past it. Except uniformed cops and a scraggly gang of undercover cops who looked more drugged and rugged than some of the people who ended up being their targets for arrest.

"Hey," Le Roy shouted, running back to the rest of the group. "Look behind those dressing room trailers."

We looked. We saw nothing at first. Then a young, average looking man walked from one of the trailers to the line of boulders at the shoreline and then down to the shoreline.

We all laughed. Heartily. The space between the water and the rocks was where we made the great majority of our arrests.

"See!" Le Roy yelled. "I been watching. Couple a guys been goin' back and forth from the trailers to the rocks. What do ya think they're doin'?" He laughed, bending at the waist for emphasis of his joy.

"Same place we're going," I remember saying.

The rocks were a cozy place for dopers at that time of night. No one could see them and these particular guys were protected by a big, high fence. No one could get to them. Except a group of not-suspicious looking dudes who obviously had business back there—you know, because of the concert and all—and we were welcomed to join them.

Well, Le Roy was welcomed, he was the first to approach and we held back. Didn't want to seem impolite while ganging up and asking if we could party with them. Le Roy went down among them after they gleefully invited him in, he being fellow beater of the Buddha bush, as marijuana was sometimes referred to by the hipsters. It was a forgone ritual among dopers to share a bowl with a well-mannered stranger.

We waited a few minutes. Another of our guys walked closer, to get a better look. He suddenly turned and waved to us. Le Roy had done it again! He'd ruined the drug party of a bunch of druggies.

The young men quickly caught on they were at least being shagged away and they got up to leave. Le Roy grabbed a bag of pot from one of them and another undercover officer placed a handcuff on his wrist. Whoops! The fun was really over with and they began to run. We stormed them. They ran away. Trouble was, there was only one way, and that was toward the chilling blue waters of Lake Michigan.

As we later learned, they'd all been sharing pot with Le Roy, so they all knew they were being arrested. Le Roy's head bobbed in the water, next to the other unfortunates, as they tried swimming.

"Help," Le Roy yelled and a couple of our other guys—notably, not me—jumped into the lake. One guy punched Le Roy in the face. Le Roy tried hitting him back. He could not, with the water interfering. He swan out a short distance and recovered a floating, almost-sinking bag of dope. All of the violators knew they could not escape so they gave up.

All four of the men were summarily arrested. They'd all smoked the killer weed and they were all carrying more of it. Soaking wet doesn't adequately describe them. It doesn't adequately describe Le Roy and the two other undercover who came out of the water.

By this time uniformed officers knew what was going on and a nearby police prisoner wagon drove up to the area.

"What about the concert?" one of them said.

They looked at each other and at us and one of them said, "Can we still play the concert?"

Uh-oh.

Before we could answer, a young-ish, attractive woman in a bath robe was descending the stairs of one of the trailers. She was screaming. At the top of her lungs, as the old saying goes.

"Where are you taking my drummer?" She shrieked. "And my guitar players! What the fuck is going on here?!"

She walked up to one officer who was holding the arm of her drummer and tried pulling the drummer away.

"Get your ass back up those stairs and into that goddamn trailer," one of my partners said to her.

Well, he yelled it to her.

The woman turned and ran. She reached the stairs and stumbled more than once while running up to the trailer door and disappearing within.

The lead officer of our group looked at the soaking wet, handcuffed prisoners, and said, "Don't tell me."

He told us. They were members of the band scheduled to go on in five minutes. Trust me, we laughed. I mean, we laughed long and heartily. Not the band members, just us scruffy, trouble-making undercovers.

Needless to say, the concert was delayed. We all rode together in the van. Many fans knew who we were and shouted the most awful, unrepeatable things at us. We laughed all the harder.

The concert did finally go on, as the Captain on the grounds allowed the musicians to perform, and be processed afterward.

Every now and then the tune and the refrain, "I am woman!" tweets in my mind, I picture an angry woman singing on the Summerfest stage and a soaking wet group of band members behind her.

# THIRTEEN
*Candy Bar*

Field training is your *real* beginning moment as a cop. I'd been a police aide for the Milwaukee Police Department for nineteen months, been around cops and precincts and commanding officers and even close up to some people who'd been arrested for serious crimes. And then I was sworn in as a full-fledged police officer and attended four months at the police academy being trained.

The first day that I walked into the second police district on Milwaukee's south side seemed like the first of my life. I could not have felt more brand new and untested. Walking through the building's front door at 3:30 p.m. on a Sunday and then entering the general police assembly could not been more intimidating. I couldn't have felt more exposed as a nobody. At least newborns aren't aware of how naked they are.

Nobody? A cop? Yeah. The uniform identifies you as one who virtually has an infinite amount of power compared to a regular citizen, with no true understanding of what that means on your first day of work. I knew at that moment I would only understand what being a police officer meant once I'd actually committed a police act. And what would that act be? Of course, I thought of the first time I'd make an arrest. Placing your hands on a fellow human being, telling them you are under arrest while placing the cold, unrelenting steel handcuffs on their wrists. Then taking them to the lock up and slamming the door. They sit in a ten by ten room, with no choice, and you walk away to get on with your life.

That is power.

That is the key moment, the ice breaker, your baptism into your new world.

I honestly thought all of that as I walked through the assembly door of the 2nd Precinct. Took me

Four-and-a-half seconds. Maybe five. Well, I didn't think it; I felt it. And feelings are more meaningful than thoughts when you're walking blindly into the most serious environment you've ever been in.

A long high, specially constructed table, with two tops slightly tilted downward from each other, stretched more than half the length of the room. Some uniformed officers leaned against the table. Others sat on benches placed against the wall. No one looked at me, even though I was a stranger in their room. They'd been expecting me, one of the new guys reporting for duty that day.

I followed along with all of the roll call rituals, descriptions of suspects, changes in department procedure; sergeants checking each officer's work gear. The veterans went through the motions in a bored manner. I saw the other new officers who were assigned to the second precinct for their field training.

Roll call ended and everyone went to their assigned posts: supervisors to their offices and street officers rounding up their equipment go to the garage and parking lots to get into their vehicles. The sounds of shuffling feet and mundane conversations about—about anything that was going on in their lives. I did not absorb or join in with any of the chatter. I was a rookie. Rookies keep their mouths shut.

Along the way I was introduced to my FTO—Field Training Officer—who was professional and pleasant but kept to himself. We went to the squad car and he opened the passenger door for me. I was surprised and hesitant. He smiled at me and said that this was the nicest thing to expect from anyone at work. It was a first and last time thing with him. An ice breaker, a lightening of the mood. I was grateful for his easy going manner.

The 2nd Precinct is what was in 1971 a second tier area as far as the number and seriousness of crimes. The FTO was quick to mention that, but just as quick to say I shouldn't let it lull me. With police work, anything can happen at any time.

We began covering the assigned squad area—the FTO rapidly pointing out things that cops look for: the grocery store was still open, his car was parked in front of the store. In the early moments of riding in the squad it was, in a way, too much too soon. (I've spoken with many veteran officers since then and all say they were completely overwhelmed when they first hit the street.)

"Well, I got some heavy duty things planned for us tonight," Roger, the Field Training Officer said to me. "Couple of high speed car chases. A bank robbery— even though it's Sunday—and I'll let you choose one yourself."

I let out a short, polite laugh, not knowing exactly what he expected. I rolled my eyes left to glance at him. He was steering the squad car with one hand at the top of the wheel, expressionless. He did not look back at me.

I'll never forget that moment. It was my first real introduction to police officer style humor, which is to speak of major crimes as though they were unremarkable incidents. The way two people might discuss their plans to do the laundry some time that day.

I didn't understand why, exactly. It wasn't long until I myself had the hard heart that is foisted upon you by co-experiencing the disastrous moments of the victims of crime for whom you worked. It was necessary to protect yourself while you were living through informing a mother that her teenager had been killed in a car accident. It became an unfortunate habit—too often expressed in front of citizens.

"Squad twenty-seven," the dispatcher said on the police radio.

That was our squad number.

"2-7, go," Roger said into the microphone.

"They're holding a shoplifter in the drugstore on K.K. and Lincoln."

K.K. and Lincoln where cross streets in our area.

"10-4," Roger said nonchalantly and replaced the microphone on its latch on the dashboard.

"That's back the other way," he said, pulling to the curb before wheeling the car around. "Sounds like you're gonna get your first arrest."

Of course all the physical reactions available in a human body under such circumstance began to set off. But they all boil down to one word: anxiety.

"2-7," the dispatcher said again. "Better hurry it up. They say the thief is fighting."

Roger grabbed the microphone once again. "10-4" he said, turning on the siren and flashing red lights on the roof.

"Now, if this guy fights with *us*, you know how to deal with it, right?" Roger asked.

I'd been trained endlessly on how to subdue a person who was fighting. But that didn't lessen the already throbbing anxiety I'd felt. "Yeah," I said. What *else* was I gonna say?

In what seemed like seconds we arrived at the drugstore at the corner of K.K. and Lincoln.

"Follow me," Roger said when we arrived and parked.

It was a small shopping area and people stopped to watch.

"No-o-o!" we heard a girl's voice shouting.

Geez, what was going on?

A man was trying to hang on to a young girl, who we later learned was nine years old.

She was squirming and trying to sink down from his arms. Roger grabbed her, as did I. She stopped for the most part, but still struggled and tried to break free. We took her out to the squad. She struggled all the way. More people had come by and were stopped and watching.

It was all phony resistance; putting on the show of not wanting to cooperate. But we both held her as we forced her to the squad. While putting her in the back seat of the squad a man's voice said from behind us, "This is what she was after."

We turned to look. He was holding a chocolate candy bar.

While driving to the precinct she screamed and kicked the back seat. "I did not steal!" she shouted.

We stopped at a stop sign. She grabbed the door handle, attempting to exit.

"Put these on her," Roger said, handing me his handcuffs.

I was turned around in my seat, on my knees. She kicked at my face. More false resistance. She stopped instantly as I put a cuff on one of her wrists.

The precinct had only been blocks away. We arrived and she stopped her resistance.

"You guys got her!" the desk sergeant yelled when we came through the front door. He came around quickly and leaned down to study her face. "Yeah, she's the one. Been missing from her aunt's house overnight."

In the conference room I studied her while Roger took her statement. Her eyes were—blank. Cold, but unemotional would best describe them. She badly needed a bath, her clothes were dirty. All of the fight had gone out of her and she admitted taking the candy bar without hesitation.

She didn't care. Didn't care that she'd be gone from her aunt's for more than a day, that she'd stolen something and that she'd struggled with cops. She was a young soul headed for trouble.

The sergeant told us after we'd finished that she wasn't going back to her aunt's, or back home, for that matter.

"They gotta keep her away from her old man. They say he likes to play slap and tickle with her, if you get my meaning."

Unfortunately, we did.

# FOURTEEN
## The Sleepers

New York cops are the best! Well, at least two of them I met around 1975 are the best. Or were, back then. They came roaring into Milwaukee one day, subpoenaed to the south east Wisconsin Federal District Court for a major drug trial regarding a crime that began in their fair city. It's not uncommon for big city narcs to get involved with federal drug cases and then be subpoenaed all over the country because of a sprawling drug dealing ring.

It was in the summer and we often needed to work different shifts. Well, they weren't really shifts, they were time allotments handed out according to the need of the department. Maybe there was a wee hour raid scheduled. Or an early morning roust and arrest of sleeping people wanted on warrants. Often times I'd process drug evidence—testing and then providing the initial probable cause that it was an illegal substance. Plenty of court in the morning and work at night for those and other reasons.

But cases in other cities, across the nation? Not so much. I had two: one in Cincinnati to pick up a prisoner and once to testify in Chicago. But New York was the gateway to the New World and all the drugs criminals could cart, carry and conspire to sell.

My partner and I were still in the office around 4:00 p.m. when two of the scruffiest looking street dudes you ever saw came into our office. We were in the back and unknown people had to be screened. These guys looked like they'd flunk every policeman screening test you could ever think up.

They were perfect.

The detective in charge said to me and my partner: "You guys are hereby off duty. Get my meaning? We need you to show these fine New York detectives around our city. They'll be testifying at the federal building on a New York heroin caper and they got here a day early."

Now, what he meant was we were to make sure the two refined gentlemen went to the right places and didn't get involved in any unnecessary kinds of activity, which would cause problems for the Milwaukee police authorities who would have to explain everything later. Follow me so far? My partner and I happened to be considered experts at going to all the right places to which I am referring, taking visiting officers with us, and making sure nothing went wrong. After all, we were blue bloods all the time. Right?

We couldn't have been happier to help our East Coast brothers of the law. They couldn't have been happier than to be with two enthusiastic undercover officers who knew all the right places for people who looked the way we did. We hit the streets together. My partner was driving—a disgusting old, beat up vehicle. We were pretending to drink liquor in order to feel more at ease.

After all, we were now off duty. So, we could pretend to drink. Okay?

We exchanged so-called police war stories and I laughed until I thought my sides would split. All of the business people to whom we introduced the New York narcs were impressed. We went from place to place, showing the New York guys our town. Things were going great. By nine o'clock we'd all pretended to drink about a ton of booze each. One of the New York guys was enjoying himself so much he was speechless. Literally. We were really tired by the end of the evening and the New York narcs were lucky they could sleep late the next day.

And then it happened.

We had the need to place ourselves on duty to deal with an illegal drug emergency. I know that sounds strange. Well, it was. It was going on 10:00 p.m. And we all needed to be going home. But my partner remembered an extremely important meeting he had with a leader of a notoriously criminal motorcycle gang on the east side of the city. The man was a leader of the lawless gang with a national reputation for serious criminal activity—like buying and selling illegal drugs—and we'd been waiting to take him down for a long time. My partner and the captain of the Narcotics Squad were quietly—secretly—waiting for the break, and my partner's informant had called the office to tell my partner that Mr. Big Shot motorcycle guy was waiting to see my partner at a hell-hole tavern on East Brady Street. He was going to do business.

"What are you going to do with the New York guys?" the detective in charge said to me over the phone. "You can't take them with you, you know."

"Of course," I said, ringing off.

"How are we gonna take these guys with us?" my partner asked when I got back to his car after using an outdoor public phone booth. Remember them? The two New York undercovers sat quietly in the back seat. Actually, one of them had fallen asleep and the other one forgot which language he spoke. Or something like that.

"No problem," I said. "We'll just go to the joint, you'll go into the place and score the dope and I'll be waiting with them, a block away in the car."

"That's not what you were told, was it?" my partner said.

"Are they armed, by the way?" I replied.

My partner and I searched and found a high caliber revolver on each of them. One of them got out of the car—I'm leaving out exactly how he got out of the car—and proudly pulled open his jacket. Sure enough, the big-ass gun was in its holster on his hip.

We were on Wisconsin Avenue, Milwaukee's main downtown street, so we got a good, well-lighted look at his piece. Traffic whizzed by the whole time.

We decided it was a go. We drove to Milwaukee's not-so-distinguished lower east side, haven of the remnants of the hippie counter culture. One of the guys had fallen fast asleep, if you get my meaning, so we decided to leave him in the back seat. The livelier of the two wanted to help as much as he could, like come into the bar with us and watch our backs.

We decided against that plan.

And Mr. Big Shot motorcycle dude only knew my partner, so I and the New York narc would have only created anxiety for him.

We parked the car on a side street two blocks from the tavern. We checked the sleeping New York narc. He was still alive. The more-or-less fully awake New York narc insisted on getting out of the car. He had to pee. The tree next to us was a fine target. And then—uh-oh—he decided he'd rather not get back in the car.

Change of plans.

Originally, I was going to sit on the cement steps of a closed resale shop across the street from the tavern, while my partner went in to buy the heroin. That changed to me *and the New York narc* sitting together on the cement steps of the old resale shop. He wouldn't leave my side and was getting more and more—sleepy.

By the time we got to the steps, we were carrying the

New York narc. It was okay, he wasn't a real big guy. We sat him down and I sat with him while my partner went across to the tavern.

We waited on the steps. And waited. And waited. At first a soft snoring sound joined us—coming from the oh-so-tired New York narc—and then it grew. And grew. And grew.

The area was a hub-bub of partiers walking from tavern to tavern. Some of them walked past us and laughed. I'll never forget two young women who sneered as they passed, with one of them saying, "Tough to pass out right on the street."

I smiled and nodded. *No, it isn't* I did not say.

After a while my partner finally came out of the tavern and started walking toward where we'd parked his car—in a direction opposite of me!

I shook the New Yorker and he actually came awake. A little. I leaned to his ear and told him in a stern voice that he had to walk as best as he could, because the deal was done. He actually did all he could to help me lift and then walk him to our car.

All was well. My partner had scored half an ounce of smack, our two guests slept quietly in the back seat and we drove off.

"I'll process the dope in the morning and these two can sleep at my place," my partner said while dropping me off at my car near the police headquarters building.

I wondered if anyone but an experienced cop would ever believe my story. I still wonder.

# FIFTEEN
*Johnny and Frank*

Sometimes the whole truth about a crime never reaches the police. At least, not in an official way.

I was on my way to Headquarters minutes before the end of my shift when a shooting was reported on the police radio. I picked up the dash microphone and told the dispatcher I was responding. The shooting was in my assigned area of responsibility and even though the normal policy was to send detectives from the succeeding shift, I responded anyway.

I was not the first officer to arrive. Several uniformed officers had arrived first, and there was one other detective who'd also extended his duty, rather than go home. We weren't surprised to see each other; we were among those who often worked late.

We worked in a very busy area.

A uniformed officer directed us to the rear door of an old, dilapidated duplex in the middle of an extremely tough part of the city. We ran up the stairs to the second floor kitchen where a bright light glared overhead. Two portly young women in nightgowns sat at the kitchen table. One was weeping, the other sat with her head down, her chin tucked into the palm of her extended hand. She looked dazed.

The officer began explaining the crime scene to us while we continued walking through the kitchen.

The floor was covered with broken glass shards. Two very small children—no more than three or four years old—tried coming into the kitchen from their bedrooms, which were located to the side. From the cuts on their feet and blood stains on the floor, it was evident they'd already been successful.

Just beyond the kitchen, in a dark living room, lay a dead man. He was face up, his arms extended and close to his sides. His jaw was open and a smashed pair of glasses lay askew on his face.

"He took a couple in the ten spot," one officer said. The ten spot meant the center mass area of his chest; it's what the firearms instructors called it because it is marked that way on the silhouette targets.

The officer finished explaining his part in the investigation while the other detective on the scene and I began doing our parts.

The children were playing in their bedroom, which was next to the living room; about ten feet from the dead man's remains. They unexpectedly broke free and into the living room and got as close to the body as they could.

"Johnny Mack, he dead?" one of the girls asked while leaning as close to the body as she could.

"Johnny Mack dead," her small companion said immediately.

"Yeah, baby, Johnny Mack is dead," one of the women called out from the kitchen. "You know that. Now get back in your room!"

The police photographer arrived and took photos. A detective lieutenant came by and we explained our investigation to him. He nodded while we spoke and walked back down the stairs.

Suddenly, a commotion arose from the back yard as a car pulled into the parking lot. Men's voices could be heard, shouting that the killer was in the back seat. The other detective and I began to go down the steps when a uniformed officer told us that it was the suspect, that he'd left the apartment immediately after the shooting, but had called for the police to come to where he was and pick him up.

Some neighbors were aware of the situation and came out of their homes to yell at the man.

I went back to the kitchen and saw the little girls had succeeded in leaving their bedroom once again and had sliced the bottoms of their feet even more on the broken glass laying on the kitchen floor. Neither of the women had moved from their chairs, or said anything to the children. I looked beyond the kitchen and saw that a dark colored kitten had gotten up on Johnny Mack's chest, sat down and was licking the body's face.

That was all I could stand.

In a loud voice I instructed the women to tend to the children, call to the cat so it would get off of the dead body and at least pretend like they were concerned with everything that was going on. The once crying woman, who had obviously been feigning her grief, began muttering something about "mothers" and "ho's" and what-have-you while she got up, stepped gingerly on the broken glass and went to the girls.

We finished our part with the crime scene. The photographer was packing up his camera, the medical examiner's people were bringing a gurney into the kitchen and headed toward the body. I had grabbed a broom and swept a clear path through the broken glass so they could do their job.

The women gave their statements about what had happened in between moments of us clearing out the kids and getting the cat off of the dead man.

"Frank said, 'Johnny Mack, don't keep comin' up on me! Don't keep comin' up on me!'" one of the women explained.

Frank was the shooter who'd run from the place. Johnny Mack hadn't listened and Frank shot him at point blank range. He stumbled into the living room where he fell and died. Frank ran. The police arrived. Frank and Johnny Mack had been jealous lovers of one of the women and it came to murder.

That's what we were told, but that ain't exactly how it happened. Not by a long shot—pun intended.

We instinctively knew we were being lied to while we investigated and figured we'd question people at police headquarters and get to the bottom of it all.

We did not.

The women both said they were playing cards at the kitchen table when Johnny Mack came over to visit. They were sitting and chatting and drinking refreshments when there was a knock on the door. It was Frank. He'd followed Johnny Mack because he was jealous and the two men had a confrontation resulting in Mr. Mack's shooting death.

The officers were checking the records of Johnny Mack and Frank while I and the other detective spoke with the women. Johnny Mack, who was in his mid-forties, had a lengthy felony record going back to his youth. Burglaries. Robberies. Prison time.

"He's a drug dealer," one of the uniformed officers said softly. He later said he'd known Johnny Mack from investigating in the area. "He was a really bad guy."

I looked at both of the women, who'd overheard the officer's remark, and neither would look back at me.

"Well," I said. "What' about Johnny Mack and his drug dealing?"

Neither woman answered. One of them shrugged.

"And how come Frank came over and broke up your card game and murdered Mr. Mack?" I inquired further.

They said nothing.

The crime scene investigation was complete, the body had been hauled away and we left the women with the broken, bloody glass on the bloody floor and the bloody children.

Outside in the back yard a small group of officers, uniformed and plain clothes, stood talking and laughing among themselves. The lieutenant was still there, smiling, relaxed. It was case closed.

"Good job," he said to all of us.

Good job, my ass. These men had collided; one had killed the other as nonchalantly as two year olds throwing temper tantrums in a sandbox. When they were done fighting, it was all over, and no one cared. If anything, they were bored and felt imposed upon by our presence. We dragged the bloody mess away, along with a killer, and it was just another shooting-killing in the neighborhood.

No big deal.

The women showed up at the District Attorney's office the following morning. They were wearing informal dresses, the kind of things one would wear while doing work out in their garden. One of them carried a royal blue velveteen Royal Crown whiskey bag for a purse. You could tell she was proud of it when she sat at the D.A.'s desk.

Frank was charged with manslaughter—using too much force in self-defense. Johnny Mack was being sliced up in the morgue. Out in the hallway a middle aged African American man dressed in a long black, leather coat and a wide brimmed hat approached me.

"Johnny Mack was the father of one of the girls and Frank is the father of the other," he said without being asked any questions. "They used to come get the welfare checks from the mothers on the first of every month, so they could cash and keep them."

He seemed disgusted.

I was mildly surprised, having heard virtually every hideous story imaginable.

"First one of them to get there got the checks, the other one got nothing," the man said.

This time they got there at the same time. Bang-bang.

"What about the women and the girls?" I asked.

He laughed. "The women got what they deserved, if you ask me." He turned and walked away.

A lot more was going on with that story. A whole lot more.

I'd decided to let him go. There was no proof of what he told me, but I was a hundred percent certain that he'd known and told me the truth. Later, I told the other detective on the case who said he'd talk to the women about it and let me know if they verified the story. Nothing more was ever said to me.

I was in the hallway outside the D.A.'s office when the women left together, after giving their statements. Their backs were toward me. They were giggling. The one with the Crown Royal purse playfully swatted the other with it.

They continued walking together, down one of the darkest hallways I'd ever seen.

# SIXTEEN
## *Mom*

Parts of Milwaukee's most derelict inner city areas have homes that were built in the early to middle 20th century. They were, and remained as of the 1980s, beautiful buildings—at least by outward appearances. Their property values had fallen to a shockingly low amount because of the crime and other negative aspects of their surroundings. There were some enterprising and rising young people who rented, and even managed to purchase, some of these homes. They had the courage to make good things happen and stood their ground.

Many of these people are well-to-do business people, or public officials in highly advanced positions. They went to school, got their university degrees, and became champions of their old neighborhoods, as well as estimable leaders of Milwaukee's society. They were always good citizens and kept to themselves, living good lives, raising their families in a responsible manner.

As a young cop and detective, I was privileged to meet many of them and proud to become friends with some. Many of them were fellow police officers and squad partners.

One of the aforementioned homes contained a family consisting of a young woman in her early thirties and two young boys around the ages of ten and twelve. This young woman and her two boys are among the most memorable people I met while on the police force.

It was cold the night I met them on Christmas Eve. My partner and I were sent to follow up on a routine burglary—there's really no such thing, but through sheer number of occurrences, they get mashed into a mundane grouping—and were greeted at the door by a young and beautiful woman who was dressed in expensive looking business attire. She smiled when she opened the door.

She motioned for us to enter, swung her arm behind her and pointed at a lonely Christmas tree. I say lonely because it was Christmas Eve and there were no presents under the tree. Or nearby. Of course, all of the presents had been taken by filth-of-the-Earth thieves who'd broken into the home of a single mother while she was out to dinner with her two sons.

We learned all that and more while interviewing her about the break-in of her home.

"Lived in this house all my life," she said. She was proud and she deserved to be. It was one of those swanky two story brick buildings made of heavy brown brick. The interior was clean and had plush, well-cared for furniture. Except for the evidence of ransacking the burglars had done while looking for children's toys to steal, the woman was obviously high-minded and cared for her family.

She was divorced and her ex-husband was not part of her children's lives. She did not elaborate.

"I'm a law clerk," she said and named an upscale law firm with a good reputation. "Wanna be a lawyer. Someday I will be."

Her appearance and demeanor were startling. She lived in a very tough neighborhood where most people lived in minimal ways. There was crime all around and it was not a restful place. Yet she was formidable against the environment—she seemed to be taking this horrible event, with horrible holiday season timing, completely in stride.

Her sons were in their bedrooms when we first arrived. After she provided the initial required information and described what had been touched and told us what had been taken, she paused and looked at me with a sad smile. She said that being a cop I must have seen this kind of thing all the time. But this time was different. Her heartache hung with me longer than a victim's pain normally did—longer than I cared to feel.

I couldn't believe what I'd heard. We were all together in the midst of a devastating event on Christmas Eve—she made sure to mention of being a Christian or that God has His mysterious ways—and she was the strongest one among us.

She called her sons to come speak with us. The younger one had been crying, the older of the two simply looked depressed.

"They got everything," the older boy said.

We looked in their bedrooms—their mother could actually afford to provide separate bedrooms for them—and saw the typical extra ransacking given to nicer homes. Pulling clothes down from their closet racks for no other reason than for the criminal to show their disdain for people who properly take care of themselves.

My partner checked for prints. That's right, in the olden days detectives themselves carried their own forensics kits and dusted appropriate items for fingerprints. CSI? What? The boys down at the lab analyzed what we mostly brought to them. Things changed very quickly.

The young mother continued searching different areas of the home, for ransacking damage as well as additional missing items. Her sons moped. Who could blame them?

So here we had an ambitious woman fighting it out in what was still largely a man's world, and doing so successfully in a respectable, decent paying career, living in a home she'd inherited but was still paying a mortgage. Raising two kids. She was winning in the losing-est area one could find.

Not good enough.

Creeps had to metaphorically smash her teeth in on the most important religious holiday of the year, according to her beliefs, and she had to quietly sift through the wreckage, keep her kids calm and contemplate her immediate future.

Every now and then I investigated a crime where a particular victim's plight gave me extra pause. This was one of those occasions, as my own spirits sank the longer I was there. Of course, cops are human and this happens to us all, although being professionals we keep it under wraps.

The woman had bravely maintained her tough-but-controlled demeanor, even making a few jokes. I stood in the dining room, writing notes in my memorandum book and went to the kitchen. She'd gone in there moments earlier and I had a question.

She was leaning against the sink counter top, with one hand stroking her chin. Her expression was blank but she stared straight ahead. She'd paid me no mind when I first entered the room. A single, thick tear streak slowly rolled down her cheek. Her eyes bulged slightly with moisture. She became aware of my presence and brought her hand to the rebellious tear streak and wiped it clean away. She looked at me, her expression dark and her features sagging, her eyes blank. Not teary and sad, but blank.

She instantly straightened and her facial expression followed suit. The tear was gone, as was the defeated expression, and she actually smiled at me.

"So, what's next?" she asked, obviously not to inquire about my duties, but to help her break the spell that had come over her.

I was shocked into silence, momentarily unable to

comprehend her strength, her fortitude, her diligence at wanting to take care of things: her kids, her wrecked home and ruined Christmas celebration. A moment later she was looking and acting the same way she'd looked and acted when my partner and I first came into her home.

That moment was among the most powerful and memorable of any I'd experienced in my police career. I never forgot the visual details, the feelings of sorrow I felt coming from her—and being dissolved by her in an instant.

Back to business, you guys have a crime to solve. I'll take care of myself, I could almost hear her thinking.

And I'd thought I was a tough guy.

# SEVENTEEN
*Spy vs. Spy*

I was twenty-three years old and had already had a more diverse career than many police officers have during their entire time on the job. All because I'd worked undercover for a year-and-a-half; mostly investigating narcotics dealers, but also some with the commercial gambling crowd, which was still illegal in Wisconsin in 1971. Prostitutes, and men fondling their own genitals in public areas, and the private parts of other men who were so inclined, also took some of my investigative time.

My father, a WWII naval veteran and a person who was raised in the first half of the 20th century, would look at me with both fear and sadness in his eyes when I explained my Vice Squad duties to him. Never said much, just stared and leaned away a bit, his thoughts obviously the kind he could never express to me, or anyone else, for that matter. But I digress.

One early weekend evening, just after roll call, my partner and I were cruising our assigned squad area. I had returned from plain clothes duties to regular police patrol a month or two earlier. Within minutes of hitting the street we saw a motorcycle gang, wearing its full colors, riding together on a street leading to the freeway. The gang was nationally famous with many crimes—including murder—attached to its resume. We automatically began following them and notified the dispatcher.

They were going the speed limit, but started revving

their engines and mufflers when they saw us. Paying their respects to their mortal enemies. The group stopped at a red light, with us right behind them. From what seemed to be nowhere an additional bike rider came up behind us, at a high rate of speed, and joined the back end of the group.

"That's speeding," my partner said.

"We didn't clock him," I said.

"So what? He was clearly driving too fast for conditions." He laughed and swatted at me. "We'll both testify in court to that. Right?"

I said right, because it was exactly what we'd do. I was just wondering if I or my partner would be signing the citation. I jest: he was the senior man, it was his all the way.

The stop light turned green and the bikers began to move. My partner put on the red lights, intending to pull the speeder over. Without looking back, the group stopped and opened a pathway for the speeding, dilatory rider, to let him roll through to the front. They then closed ranks. The gang began rolling slowly, with us following them. My partner leaned on the siren.

I watched the speeding biker when he got to the front, and he took off like a bullet to get onto the freeway. His gang buddies spread wide, to block our path, and we watched the offender light it up to eighty or ninety miles per hour on the freeway. We could not get through to him. My partner called for assistance over the police radio, and the dispatcher called for a city-wide officer back up to come to our aide.

The group of bikers slowly moved along on the freeway, and the violator we'd been pursuing was long out of sight. The gang then began to speed up.

"Goddamn sonsabitches!" my partner yelled. "They're all going to jail for interfering with us."

Meanwhile uniformed squads with their led lights

flashing and their sirens blaring began arriving at the scene. The bikers were sly. They cautiously moved to the side of the road, feigning an effort to let properly allowed emergency vehicles to pass.

Guess what?

We pulled over to the first biker, who calmly sat on his motorcycle. We ran toward him.

"Can I help you, Officer?" the scruffy looking man with proud outlaw style colors on his vest politely asked as we approached him.

"You can turn around and put your hands behind your back," my partner said. He motioned for me to put handcuffs on him.

"Anything you say, Officer," the biker said in an exaggerated polite tone.

I clicked the cuffs on him and he stood silently, without offering any resistance. I look ahead on the freeway and squads were arriving at breakneck speed. Each biker calmly turned around as officers approached and put their hands behind their backs. They were immediately handcuffed.

"Wow," the biker in our custody said. "Must be big trouble in the city."

He smiled slightly. My partner was furious, but treated him properly. Many citizens had stopped their cars and come out of nearby homes to watch the goings on. The police radio blasted with officers informing the dispatcher of their arrests of motorcycle riders, stretching a quarter mile ahead of us.

"Your buddy must have a ton of warrants, for you guys to let him through like that," my partner said.

The biker leaned toward us with an exaggerated quizzical expression. "Excuse me?" he said in the most polite-but-condescending tone one could imagine.

About two blocks ahead we saw one biker take a swing at a detective who'd joined the chase.

"Goddamnit!" the man we had in custody said.

The detective quickly punched the biker, and the biker fell down.

"Ain't supposed to be like that," the biker said angrily.

Eventually all of the motorcycle riders were placed in prisoner wagons or the rear seats of properly equipped squad cars. Tow trucks began arriving to remove the motorcycles.

At the 2nd Precinct all of the motorcyclists were being processed for obstructing an officer.

Then it happened.

I walked into the cell block, in which more than twenty biker prisoners were being held, and I saw him. "Him" was a man I'd used as an informant less than six months earlier when I was working undercover on the narcotics squad. He stood leaning against the cell door and looked at me.

He recognized me first! Me, clean shaven and with short-short hair, wearing a police uniform, and the druggie, drunkard biker guy knew who I was before I knew who he was.

It made no difference; we'd scoped each other out, a la *Spy vs Spy*. I stopped and stared, and he stared right back. His eyebrows arched in the center, and a few moments later the look of genuine fear smudged his face. I smiled. He cowered. Here he was, a rough and tough motorcycle gangster—in one of the most notorious, violently criminal and even murderous motorcycle gangs in the country—who was exposed as nothing more than a simpering, sniveling snitch for the po-lice. It just had to burn at him: the code of the gangs is to never squeal on anyone—unless, I guess, it doesn't hurt you or yours. I lingered long enough for him to step back from the cell bars and then walked away.

We wrote reports and each biker was eventually

cuffed and marched to a squad car or prisoner wagon, for the journey to headquarters downtown where the processing would be completed.

Biker boy had introduced me to a well-known prescription drug thief and dealer, who sold me a large amount of drugs.

"Don' you worry 'bout Peter," the biker had said at the time. "He figures you for The Man and I'll lunch him myself." He spoke in a heavy southern drawl.

The drug deal had been one of many similar ones, which had all clustered together in my mind. After arresting the criminal biker snitch, the drug deal separated itself into the group of memorable drug deals I'd been involved with. It remains that way to this day.

Eventually the biker snitch was led from his cell to a squad in the police garage. He had to wait a moment before being seated. I walked to where he stood and looked at him, with no expression on my face. He knew I hadn't burned him with his buddies, but I knew he'd worried about exactly what I'd do the whole time he sat in that cell.

"Thanks," he whispered and lowered his eyes, his hands cuffed behind his back, his shoulders slumped when he eventually shuffled ahead. I stayed at his side and walked along with him every step, but he would not look at me.

I opened the squad car door for him. He sat and continued staring straight ahead.

Post Script: the original biker we'd tried to pull over was identified several weeks later. He was from Indiana and was wanted on a murder warrant, which is why his fellow gang members blocked us from getting to him. He was eventually arrested and received a life sentence. I heard a long time afterward he'd been paroled after serving more than ten years in an Indiana prison.

# EIGHTEEN
## *JonBenet Ramsey*

You are a small town police officer—Boulder, Colorado, home of the late JonBenet Ramsey—serves as a good example. Therefore, you have never investigated a major crime, which is expected. Major crimes don't occur in small towns. At least not the type of major event programmed into the minds of average Americans. You may be the type of officer who peers into every possibility, as though it could actually be the real deal. You could be the type who socializes with business owners and regular citizens more than anything. Who knows? *Because there never will be a real crime in your little 'burb.*

None of your town's founders even thought about that. Why would they? Town founders are talented, mature leaders of people. Businessmen. Businesswomen. Their associates and supporters are of the same mind as they take care of you and your business and take care of others. Squeeze in some fun. Live a good life.

Major crimes? You mean like *Law and Order* on TV? Very entertaining. Thank goodness it's as close as the average person ever gets to witnessing crime drama.

It's the way good people live, and the people you work for are the epitome of good.

Of course, you, the small town officer, will have things to do: issuing parking tickets, directing traffic during city-wide events, following businessmen carrying their bags of daily sales to the bank. The *major* crimes: locking up the stereotypical town drunk. The major laws are made at the state level. You'd be on the scene of those things too, *if they ever occurred in our little 'burb.* State and Federal law enforcement officers handle that, and they are more like rumors than real people. Even to you, the small town officer.

Then one day...

You are sent to the home of the wealthy John and Patsy Ramsey, who report that their six-year-old star, model, actress, beautiful beyond belief daughter, JonBenet, has been kidnapped.

Kidnapped from their home, a large, beautiful, expensive residence located where other wealthy people live.

You've had minimal training in complex, felonious crimes—if any—and, again, you've never *investigated* any. This is not a criticism, you've done exactly what you were hired—and trained—to do.

And you are it. On your way, going in, you know that you are *it.*

Upon arrival you are told suspicious, pat tale by the little girl's parents, who seem too calm. The girl was put to bed the previous evening at 9:30 p.m. in her upstairs room. The parents went to bed shortly after that. The mother says that shortly after 5:00 a.m. the next morning, she got up and went downstairs, where she found a ransom note on the steps.

The note says her daughter has been taken from their home and will be killed in twenty-four hours unless the perpetrators are given over one hundred thousand dollars. They will be called with further instructions, but no call is ever received. The mother and father check their daughter's bed and find it empty.

9-1-1 is called at 5:25 a.m. You arrive seven minutes later. The note said that the kidnapper(s) will call. The police wait with the parents; no call ever comes.

What do you do?

You continue investigating, of course. Your original suspicion of the too-calm parents and the relative ease with which the kidnapping was alleged to have been accomplished remains. But you make no accusations at that time. Remember, you've had minimal to no detailed training or experience in matters of this magnitude. Brings you back to...

...*what do you do?*

First, you call your commanding officer, who has had more investigation experience than you. Right? Except, well, let's imagine that that's not the case. There are myriad reasons why that could be. It happens. Believe me, it happens.

There are basic things—common sense things—that every cop is trained to do. Things thoughtful non-police officers could arrive at through simple common sense.

But this is where things went wrong. And the reason why JonBenet was found murdered in her own home many hours later on December 26th, 1996.

In fact, proper police procedures were, how shall I say, nuked. The scene was not sealed or searched, random neighbors and friends were allowed to enter the home.

I know. It is hideous.

As was previously stated, the officers were indeed correct to be suspicious of the parents' story. That someone had forcibly—but so soundlessly the parents were not awakened—entered their home in the dark of night, proceeded to their daughter's bed and just as soundlessly removed her from the home. Said kidnappers also brought a note and left it in the house for the parents, and then the police and forensics experts, to examine.

But I'm getting ahead of myself.

Making no sound while entering the home is not a big deal. Expert lock pickers can do that.

Knowledgeable people could also immediately silence the child, even before removing her from her bed.

*Aside*: leaving a note at the scene is a very bad idea, for the reasons already pointed out. But it is possible, even if not plausible.

Now, even you, the small town officer, knows the entire property is a crime scene. Right? And that given the magnitude of this particular investigation, said crime scene must be sealed off and searched inch-by-inch for any possible clues. Right? Start with the building—from the daughter's bed outward you go to every single place, from the attic to the basement. Everything is photographed. Every possible bit of evidence is properly handled and recovered.

*Attic to basement.*

Uh-oh.

The basement. JonBenet Ramsey is found hours later, dead in a basement closet. *Hours later.*

Forget about miniscule, trace evidence possibilities. Forget about the lack of observable forced entry.

The dead body of a six-year-old daughter in a basement closet is something the initial investigating officers must locate. They must recover it within minutes of their arrival upon the scene.

Think deeper. Wouldn't Mom and Dad check those spots themselves; from the instant they knew there was a problem? Especially easily accessible places: under beds, inside closets. *Let's hope against hope that this is a horrible, stupid joke* world cross their minds. Panic stricken parents would literally rip the place apart the more they came to believe that their child had indeed been kidnapped. That it was not some sort of hoax.

All before they even call the authorities.

Wouldn't it?

That child's body *should* have been recovered by Mom and Dad before 6:00 a.m. And that's giving a lot of extra time from 5:25 a.m.

Even if they were too panicked and confused to check the basement, they would have been screaming—and crying—hysterically when the police arrived. Demanding the officers immediately pull out all stops.

Wouldn't they?

Yeah, they would have.

Times infinity, as it is often expressed these days.

Oh well, at least the original investigating officers *thought* the case was dubious. Acting on their suspicions, automatically doing routine police work? Not so much.

In fact, it wasn't until early afternoon when a detective asked a neighbor—*a freakin' neighbor!*—to accompany the father to the basement, to search for anything unusual, and the girl was found in a closet, covered by a blanket.

She'd been hit on the head and strangled and had obviously been placed there before Mrs. Ramsey got out of bed and found a ransom note on the stairs leading to the second floor. No need to challenge that possibility.

From that point forward the matter instantly grew into one of the most morbidly insane incidents in America's crime history. The bizarre litany of subsequent events is well-documented: Mom is a suspect, Dad is a suspect, both declare their innocence. After a grand jury finished deliberation in 1999 they provided their recommendation to the District Attorney, who sealed the case and proceeded no further, without explanation.

Go figure.

Okay, I will. The investigation was so fouled up no D.A. could have presented accumulated evidence to a jury and then reasonably hoped for a conviction.

The lack of intense follow up; the fact that no possibility of an outside perpetrator was officially presented until years later.

The grand jury result was made public in—2013? Of course, the D.A. had righteously feared he did not have enough evidence to issue charges.

An interesting addendum to the case is the confession to the break in and murder of JonBenet made by a man who had been a school teacher and who had been convicted of possessing child pornography, given many years later, while he was living in Thailand. Forget the details: it was nothing more than a very bad joke.

The police investigation can best be summed up in one word: failure—with an infinite number of exclamation points.

And that's being kind. Volumes could be written describing the outrageous incompetence of all involved, going all the way back to those who developed the town from the ground up. You must have a system for effectively dealing with crimes—from spitting on the sidewalk to the murder of JonBenet Ramsey.

That things went so far out of control is a monstrous disgrace to the tradition of law enforcement.

# NINETEEN
## *Blood Dude*

If it weren't for dealing with unexpected, crazy and very often dangerous events, police work would simply be another pencil pusher's cozy affair with the working public. Though quite obvious, it is virtually never considered when people evaluate a police officer's job. It involves looking things up, writing things down, sending information to other agencies and the like. In fact, there is a division of that type within every police department in America—the Inside Crew. Many are officers recovering from injuries before they can be released for street duty.

I spent my own time doing this work after spraining an ankle while chasing a juvenile thief. It was my first assignment with the Milwaukee Police Department as a police aide. I learned a lot and it was the foundation of my career.

But once you're sworn in as a police officer and are qualified to hit the streets to enforce the law, it is quite obviously a different business. Depending on the areas and neighborhoods you work in it can be slow and leisurely and relatively calm. Citizens in quiet, mostly crime-free neighborhoods deserve on-the-spot service, the same as those who live in, ah, busier areas.

My lot in life was to be a busy cop. I liked it. There were dangerous and sad and strange moments. It was the crazy times which raised eyebrows and offered looks of disbelief given you by those to whom you explained your story. Most of them happened when I worked on the Vice Squad. The Vice Squad is by nature Crazy Town. I've cited several examples. But one crazy deal occurred while I was a detective investigating major crimes—dressed in a business suit and tie. A small group of uniformed officers was there with me and my partner. And it was like nothing else I'd ever experienced as a cop.

It was nighttime in a busy, wild-assed criminal infested neighborhood, in the heart of the inner city. To put it plainly, and perhaps even a bit rudely, people with enough money fled the inner city and moved to the suburbs. People who were broke were stuck in the inner city. And in our culture, being broke brings a long list of unhappy, even violent experiences, over which you have little to no control.

Anyway: nighttime. Dangerous surroundings. Calls for police crackling through the airwaves. My partner and I got our crackling call shortly after a pair of uniformed officers were sent to investigate a break in of a residential garage. But this was different. Other squads were being called for backup. That usually happened before detectives were sent to investigate.

When we arrived upon the scene several officers were standing around outside the garage, which was dark inside. Several of its windows had been smashed, with large shards sticking out from the frames. One officer standing by the side door had his gun drawn.

"Not sure exactly what this is," he said to us before we could ask. "A dude's in there, yelling to himself, throwing stuff. Look at this," he said, pointing to a remaining piece of glass still stuck in its frame. A thick, long streak of blood-stained the glass.

"Sounds like a drunk trying to do a garage burglary," my partner said.

"Exactly," the officer said. "But he's screaming and yelling that he's going to kill us all. 'Look at all the goddamn blood,' he said one time. And we did. We peeked through the window with flashlights and there's blood here," he pointed at the streak on the window before us, "but there's blood all around on the other broken windows." He pointed to the front, overhead door.

The other officers at the scene stood behind us, seemingly waiting to be told what to do.

I was confused. Why hadn't the officers forced their way in and arrested the screaming, bleeding drunk?

"He keeps saying that he's cut to pieces and that anyone who touches him will die," the officers said.

"Well, we gotta go in," one of the officers said.

Random chatter among the officers continued.

"I don't know. Dude sounds like Dracula to me."

"Got that mixed up, dude. Dracula drinks blood, he don't give blood."

"Well, that long, sharp broken window thing here. Looks like a vampire's tooth."

"Why don't you shut up?"

"Why don't you shut up?"

They chuckled. The sacred bond of blue blood shared by cops does not always kick in when engaged in juvenile banter while doing things like ginning up the nerve to arrest a drunken, bleeding and belligerent, blood demon.

Or words to that substantial affect. Cops will say anything at any time to break up the tension and this guy was going to kill anyone who touched him. Or touched his blood. Or whatever.

My partner and I stood behind the small group of uniformed officers as they prepared to enter the garage. An officer reached through the side door's broken window, found a light switch on the wall and turned on the lights. We all waited outside for the blood drunk's reaction. Nothing at first. A single car sat parked against the far wall of the two car garage. Inside the car sat a very drunk, very bloody man.

Officers pointed their guns at him as they entered. I took my turn entering. The man had come to a sitting position at the edge of the driver's side doorway. The officers had stopped their approach to assess the situation.

"Come get me, bros," the man shouted. He held out his hands. His very bloody hands, which he shook at the officers while laughing hysterically. Drops spattered through the air.

He moved out of the car and stood. His face was streaked with blood, as were his clothes. He continued laughing uproariously.

"'Fraid of a little blood, bros?" he challenged.

Of course, no one wanted to touch him. But they had to. An officer had gone to one of the squads and retrieved several pairs of vinyl gloves, which he divvied up and gave to his fellows. Two officers approached and grabbed him. He lashed out, putting up a fake resistance and attempted to have physical contact with any officer possible. He wasn't fighting or striking out in any way, just trying to touch everyone he could. He continued laughing and forced the officers to handcuff him. The rest of us moved in to help hold and push him along. He laughed and laughed.

I wondered why.

All I knew was that a few tiny drops of his blood spattered onto my clothing. Other officers had drops on their face. They struggled to get him into full custody. He continued laughing. We all looked at each other. What a fuckin mess.

Some officers conveyed him to the hospital where he was quickly examined and bandaged. By the time my partner and I arrived at the detective bureau assembly, he'd already been placed in an interrogation room.

So far, just another drunk using available weapons, like his own blood, to put on his show.

The officers were beginning their reports. Attempted burglary—a felony charge the D.A. would drop from felony status to some sort of misdemeanor, where it could be quickly disposed of in a city court.

We were sitting right outside his closed detention door. He started kicking it. Over and over. Nothing unusual. Maybe he had to use the restroom and was using some sort of code to alert us. Maybe he was lonely. A uniformed officer opened the door.

The prisoner had stripped all of his bandages from his wounds—wounds it should be stated he'd inflicted upon himself. He waved the bloody bandages at the poor officer. He'd squeezed as much blood as he could from his injuries and began flinging the droplets at anyone who approached him. Once again, it took several officers to hand cuff and restrain him.

I knew what he was doing. Later, it had dawned on us all.

"Heard of Hep C?" he shouted. "I'm a carrier! It's in my blood! Y'all have just been infected."

We all stepped back and examined ourselves. I had a few drops on my dandy new suit. Rubbed my face, my hand had a few tiny streaks of blood. One uniformed officer had a partial hand print of blood on his face. He blanched. Tears welled in his eyes.

"Hep C can kill ya!" he shouted. "I've seen it. And he's a transfer, dude," the officer said in a loud voice while pointing at the blood savage.

The bloody prisoner laughed until he doubled over and dropped to the floor. I personally wasn't fearful. I knew there was treatment. But at least one officer was truly terrorized. Others started taking off their outer garments. They examined each other's faces.

A lieutenant had been notified and came to us.

"You'll all be tested and given immunizations," he said. "Don't worry."

The officer whose face had gone whiter than the Pope's robe, sat with half of his clothing removed. He stared straight ahead. Thinking back I know he had health hang-ups. He was in deep distress.

"Worst day on the job," I heard him mutter while we all gathered our garments and filed into the restroom to scrub up.

Note: this was just before the HIV nightmare had begun in the early/mid-1980s, so we only considered the treatment for Hepatitis C.

Imagine the panic if AIDS had been on the table.

# TWENTY

## *The Sneer*

There was a master defense attorney in Milwaukee named James Shellow. He was nationally renowned and had received a lot of press during the 1960s civil rights protest era. He was also contacted quite frequently by defendants regarding controlled substance cases. Not for some tool doing a doobie in an alley, but for handling the cases of people involved with selling large quantities.

He was also magnificent with all manner of other cases—from homicides on down. And one more quirky thing: cops liked him. Mmm hmm. I wrote it; you read it. Police officers from a large city department actually liked the best defense attorney in their town. Although he truly was one of the best defense attorneys in the country, he never received the press needed to claim that stature. Acclaim went to Johnny Cochran—overrated!—F. Lee Bailey—who by all accounts was for real—and others, mostly grandstanding—er—working, on the country's West Coast.

Hollywood style.

The Kardashians' late father had also been one of these top attorneys, which he proved by his efforts in the O.J. Simpson trial. Wish he were still here, getting some of the press his kids are getting. But once again, I digress.

The reason James Shellow was liked is simple. He was fair and honest. He also had, in my opinion, a Mensa mind, so he could easily figure out the cases he handled and present reasonable solutions to his opponents. Many times the proper solution was obvious and could be handled quickly without a bru-ha-ha trial. I had many cases with him, mostly drug deals and personally know this to be true.

But there was one humdinger of a court trial that went down in everyone's book—even Mr. Shellow's, which I know because he told me—and I believe must be shared with the world.

Goes like this.

Middle of winter, late at night, in the large parking lot of a large nightclub on Milwaukee's far northwest side, some drunken twenty-somethings are arguing about an incident that had started inside the tavern. Somewhere between indoors and outdoors one of the youngsters produced a knife and stuck another guy with it. The stabber runs. Everyone runs. Except the guy who got stabbed. He's dead.

It was a literally insane crowd oriented mess of a crime scene. One of the dead man's buddies tells a story of a crazed butchery by a madman. The suspect is identified and the knife was recovered. The madman/butcher is arrested for first degree murder. Simple.

Actually, not. Others at the scene said the victim had been the biggest trouble maker there. That his eventual killer had drawn a knife—three and one half inch blade—out of genuine fear for his safety. He stuck the guy, all right, but it was a manslaughter deal, not a life-in-prison thing.

But it had made big noise in the media and the D.A.'s office apparently felt compelled to charge First Degree Murder.

As you can guess, Attorney James Shellow's services were high-end, dollar wise. But the suspect's father had high-end money, so he could afford to hire the best in the business.

Everyone in the courtroom shuttered the first day when they saw Attorney Shellow enter. This was gonna be a fist fight, a hacking-slashing thing that was going to rattle the entire courthouse. The D.A., a courageous man and a good prosecutor, was gritting his teeth. I was gritting my teeth and all I did was sit at the D.A.'s table, as his aide to fetch witnesses and reports.

The trial was about to begin. Mr. Shellow was his usual smiling, exuberant, pleasant, sell-you-your-own-shoes self. He spoke with the courtroom bailiffs and other personnel assigned to work there. They were all buddies from way back. Mr. Shellow had placed a narrow folder containing a few reports on his table. One assistant sat with him. The D.A.'s table was filled with reports, photos and the you-name-its that prosecutors need.

The trial began. Things were quickly leaning in the defendant's favor, but the original charge stood: First Degree Murder.

The key witness for the prosecution was finally called to the stand. I had taken his statement and personally had no hope that he'd help the case; he was a party animal in his early twenties who, as one old saying goes, was lucky he'd learned how to tie his own shoes. He shuffled hipster-like as he approached the witness stand, with a bit of sneer on his face.

Spoiler alert: the sneer was soon to be gone.

The D.A. matter-of-factly brought him along in his testimony. It was all about screaming and yelling and hacking and slashing and finally, the climactic moment when he pointed at the defendant and said, "He did it."

Now it was the defense's turn. Mr. Shellow approached the witness with a genuinely pleasant smile and accompanying pleasant demeanor. Before he began questioning the witness he asked the judge for the drawing board to be placed in front of the jury. The drawing board was an archaic piece of wooden, elementary school style furniture, with several large pieces of paper hanging down.

He said he liked the jury to see as much as possible, to write down statements made by witnesses if necessary, so the jurors could better focus on them; perhaps create a vision in their minds. It is a common tactic.

The witness had performed badly under direct examinations. He either misspoke or could not remember details of what he'd experienced the night of the killing. And that was still during the D.A.'s questioning, before Shellow had even begun his cross examination.

He was a trussed up turkey sitting on the table of one of the best attorneys there ever was. We all knew what was going to happen.

"So," Shellow said to the witness. "When exactly did you see the activities described in this incident?"

"On the night that it happened," said the sneering witness, who was already greatly irritated by being questioned, even in an easy going way by the prosecutor.

Shellow paused and smiled. "What night was that?"

The witness wiggled and stuttered and finally 'fessed up to not being sure. It was the impression he'd given during the easy going direct questioning. Shellow gave him more than one chance to supply the correct answer—he was actually documenting contradictory statements that he'd use against him when the time was right.

"Don't remember the day, huh?" Shellow asked, more than once.

The witness was rapidly going from frustrated to angry. His faced had reddened. The time was right.

"On some random day!" the witness finally blurted,

during a moment when Shellow wasn't even questioning him.

The D.A. tried to object, saying the witness was under extreme duress. The judge interrupted him to tell him he had no standing to interfere.

"Let me write that on the board," Shellow quickly said about the witnesses unexpected statement and wrote "On Some Random Day" in thick, black, magic marker ink on the front page. He flipped it over the top.

Mr. Shellow eventually asked—a bit sarcastically—if the witness knew the year in which the crime had occurred.

The witness did not answer. Shellow asked him again. The judge finally ordered the witness to answer Shellow's question.

The witness threw his hands up. "In some random year!" he shouted and sat back.

The courtroom grew totally quiet. I couldn't believe what the witness was doing to himself.

Shellow dutifully strode to the board and wrote the words "In Some Random Year" on the blank page and flipped it over.

After being mercilessly badgered, in the slick way good attorneys manage without being told to stop, the moron—er, witness—on the stand obviously began to detach. Finally, he interrupted Shellow and said, "I lied."

Everyone in the courtroom froze in place and grew quiet. Attorney Shellow gleefully and quickly stepped to the board and wrote in thick, black magic marker letters "I lied." He flipped the page over the top.

After a long, dramatic pause, Shellow looked toward the jury and said, "Let's examine what I believe is the essence of this witness's testimony and the underpinning of the State's case against my client."

He went to the board and flipped all of the pages back to the first one.

Mr. Shellow pointed to the page, upon which the first statement was written. He spoke the words out loud: "On Some Random Day." He used a pointer to point out each word.

The next page came over the top: "In Some Random Year," Shellow said matter-of-factly while pointing at the words he'd written.

Quickly, the last page, Shellow pointed at the words: "I lied." He said them while he pointed.

He slowly approached the jury, partially opened his suit jacket and placed his hands on his sides. He shook his head while looking down. He then looked up at the jurors, and smiled.

"On some random day, in some random year, I lied," he said in a clear, measured tone. "That, ladies and gentlemen, sums up this man's testimony."

Being the prosecutions number one witness, it also summed up their case against the defendant.

Attorney Shellow walked to the witness, stopped and stared at him with a blank expression. He looked at the judge. He turned to look at the D.A., where I too was sitting and then turned back at the jury.

"On some random day, in some random year, I lied," he repeated the witnesses words one more time for effect. "What do you think about that?" he asked, rhetorically.

The D.A. stood. "Your Honor, may I approach the bench?"

"Yes, Mr. D.A.," the judge said. "I think that you should." The judge stood, "We will take a brief recess while I speak with the assistant district attorney in my chambers." He looked at Mr. Shellow. "Care to join us, Jim?"

Mr. Shellow nodded and walked toward the judge's bench.

The witness got off the stand and walked toward the back of the courtroom. He was not sneering.

Oops. I already told you that.

# TWENTY-ONE
## *M.E.s*

Brainpower and stability are not synonymous. You could make a comparison between brainpower and many things: wisdom, knowledge, behavior—look at all the crime syndicate leaders we've had; think they didn't have Mensa minds?—and so on. Unfortunately, many people with the virtually unlimited ability to accurately figure out all manner of raw data, don't always do the right thing with their conclusions. They twist it to obtain their own, wrongful desires.

What happens when some of these people have ambition and the need for power and riches or fame, or maybe to be a doctor or a lawyer, comes into play. Huh? An uncountable number of disastrous scenarios could be thought up in an instant. As comedian Lily Tomlin once said during a skit, "Everyone from kings and presidents to the scum of the Earth can be served." Again, we could name them. When we've finished throwing up, we can hopefully get on with our lives.

As you go down the line you'll find people with big, bad brains in many places. Being a cop for thirty-two years, I came into contact with some of these people. Judges. Lawyers. Businessmen—notice how I put them last, just having a little fun. The great majority of judges and lawyers and businessmen/women are fine people. The point is, they are everywhere.

It goes without saying that if they somehow jam themselves into important positions in society, they can really hurt things. And humanity being what it is, it happens all the time.

During my time as a police officer I spent more than twenty-five years doing detective work—investigating all aberrant behavior in every area of life. Much of that time was spent investigating homicides, the most heinous of all crimes. Part of a detective's duty is to attend the autopsies of murder victims. The people conducting, or at least supervising, these examinations are physicians. No one has bigger brains than the those folks. Right?

Two different medical examiners were employed in Milwaukee during my first twenty years on the police force. They happened to be women, unusual considering the time period. They were brilliant. The first was a young, extremely attractive woman who frequently socialized with top professionals of the community. She did an excellent job and assistant district attorneys loved having her as their expert witness.

She also had a great, extremely off-beat sense of humor. She pulled off some outrageous jokes, the kind I cannot divulge here. But she is not the medical examiner to whom I'm referring as I proceed.

Another woman, who'd served some time as an assistant medical examiner, took over the position about ten years after I started my time as a police officer. Her term was a controversial time period, to say the least. She, too, had a brilliant mind, but had neither the looks nor the personality of her predecessor. Though loaded with brainpower, she was unable to consistently do her job well. When considering the stakes of the cases she was involved in, she made a lot of people, ah, nervous.

The law enforcement community was primary among those who felt on edge, since some people literally got away with murder due to her incompetence. That spread to everyone who lived in the Milwaukee area, because, of course, people who were known for a fact to be willing to kill to get what they wanted were on the loose. It eventually led to her demise, which some said could not have arrived soon enough.

She was a person with enormous brainpower but little to no stability. And it was tragic to watch her because she had started out at the top of her class. And even though she had an odd personality, she was initially well-regarded, and did her job well. She was credible as a pathologist as well as a witness in criminal court. The old joke around the Milwaukee law enforcement and District Attorney's offices was medical examiners always seemed to be a little weird. The first M.E. to whom I referred was considered a classic case in point.

But the first examiner was extremely reliable, in both her findings and her ability to come across well as an expert in her field.

The second woman was completely opposite. She could do the job, but soon began to falter. I personally did not wonder why. I watched several autopsies that she performed in order to obtain spent bullets in murdered victims. She would talk to herself in a loud voice. She had Tourette's Syndrome and would blurt swear words, no matter where she was.

Once I was riding an office elevator with her and some county supervisors and other businesspeople. The elevator was completely quiet until she yelled out "Shit!" After a lengthy, uncomfortable moment, I looked to see if something was wrong. She was smiling broadly and said nothing. She decided to use the quiet, smiling face tactic to keep from alarming people around her. It had the opposite effect. No one could talk her out of using that tactic.

More than one detective who was regularly assigned to witness autopsies spoke of her eccentric behavior while working on the cadavers. She would put her fingers on her face or in her mouth—while wearing vinyl gloves smeared with blood and other dead body tissue. Her constant explosive expletives were nonstop, even when officials from other communities were doing business at her office or in the autopsy room. She would prop herself against cadavers while taking a break. These are only bits and pieces I had heard. Many more similar occurrences had been cited.

She could do the technical part of her job, but she began making too many mistakes. Small ones could be dealt with, but city officials were growing alarmed. She quickly gained the reputation for being odd and unscrupulous people took advantage.

Some defense attorneys drew her into discussions about her work and she was more than happy to say anything that came to mind. She unwittingly divulged information with more than one defense attorney who used it to rework their approach and get a better deal for their client. Or to somehow compromise the case and get a not guilty verdict when it was not appropriate.

Word of that activity leaked to the D.A.'s office and complaints were being made. Ask a D.A. how much they enjoy re-trying a defendant when there's a mistrial when one juror was wrongly convinced to vote not guilty because of something the medical examiner had said.

Ask the drunken defense attorney celebrating loudly at a strip bar on the night they twisted a trial that was supposed to have been a slam-dunk win for the prosecution, but their guy got off instead. Said attorney developed a reputation for success in trials, along with an expanding bank account, as the result of a growing reputation of winning.

And it happened because of the mistake of an off-the-rails expert in the forensics field.

By the way, I was at the aforementioned strip club very late one night, after work and watched as the attorney enjoyed himself after his victory in court. There was no indication of how he'd done it at that time, it seemed like just a really good lawyer won a case in court. Years later that case was named as one of those suspected of having been unwittingly undermined by the witless medical examiner.

As she gained more experience and publicity, she began publicly speaking her mind about things—with bad consequences. She was on her way out of her job and she knew it. And the story goes, she began to retaliate.

A final, fatal act to terminate her job was when she publicly suggested homicide cases were in danger of being wrongly mishandled by incompetent people in Milwaukee's legal community. She supplied no verifiable proof. By this time, she was not being taken seriously by anyone in authority in Milwaukee. She left her job shortly thereafter.

She disappeared from the public. Years went by. A few people claimed they saw her walking alone on sidewalks in Milwaukee's downtown district. Though not validated, we all thought it possible.

On one night at about 2:00 a.m. officers on routine patrol were performing their nightly task of clearing areas where the homeless would camp out for the evening. She was found in a corner of a doorway at the public museum, wrapped in myriad of unmatched clothing, sound asleep. The young officers did not recognize her—she was before their time—and shuffled her along. They wrote her name on a Field Interrogation report and turned it in at the end of their shift.

Older officers at the 1st Precinct recognized her name. Word of the incident quickly spread. It has been more than two decades since she has been in

Milwaukee's news. But it had been much longer than that since she'd been in her right mind.

# TWENTY-TWO
## *Donkey BJ*

The Milwaukee lakefront drug parties that flourished in the late 1960s and early 1970s were a sight to behold. The group of people attending on weekends during decent weather were little more than a wakeful, hallucinatory bad dream. I worked undercover at dozens of them. People were there for one reason: to get high and to make connections with drug dealers for a regular supply of their favorites—from marijuana to heroin.

Unfortunately, some local community leaders, including some from the mainstream news media, didn't catch on very quickly. Instead, some of them celebrated the new style of get togethers, where young people from all over the area could go to make friends and improve their lives. The *Milwaukee Journal* had a special photo page during that era and their editors published a close-up photograph of a young man lighting a pot pipe on a sunny, Sunday afternoon at a rock concert at the lakefront.

Parents across the city couldn't believe the naiveté—sorry, I called it arrogance then and still believe that to this day—of some working at a main, national newspaper to virtually promote drug use. Swift action was called for. City leaders were embarrassed. Now, that was forty years ago and the people running the show then are gone now. Things have definitely changed.

But we undercovers were swept into action on many succeeding weekends and made literally hundreds of drug arrests. And arrests for resisting an officer. And arrests for Battery to a Police Officer. And we were criticized in so-called professional editorials for picking on the kids, when there were banks being robbed.

Speaking of photographs, one was taken of an undercover officer by the publishers of an alternative news source that emanated from the hipster side of the city. It was posted on the front page, a full page photo. The paper was available in all of the stores on the east side of the city. Threats poured in against the officer. The mainstream news sources decried such actions by lawbreakers, but the people who read the off-beat street sheets and newspapers weren't the type to follow the real news, so it had little affect among the violators.

We served a search warrant at a drug dealers house shortly afterward and the photo of the officer was posted prominently on the living room wall. The people we arrested said the picture was in all the drug houses throughout the neighborhood.

The majority of the people who consistently attended these drug parties in the parks were, obviously, of low intellect and morality. They didn't care about poisoning themselves and the only reason they cared about being arrested was because of all the hassle. We arrested many of them several times—they had come to know who we were and used drugs in front of us, anyway.

The hardcore partiers went to the parks on any given day of the week. Why not? They were shiftless, unemployed and looking for some hallucinogenic fun. During the week there were relatively small groups, but we were assigned to check them all. And by golly, we made drug arrests every time we went to the park. One group in particular hung out together in one of the smaller sections of the lakefront park, a place beneath a tall, majestic and beautiful bluff. Perfect place to fuck up. During one dismal and unbelievable streak we arrested some of the same people three times in the week—for using drugs the first time we visited and for disorderly conduct and fighting with us when we arrested them the next times we visited.

Sometimes a uniformed patrol car would drive past and notify the dispatcher of the goings on, who would then notify the narcotics squad. Then off we'd go. Upon arrival we'd always be amazed at seeing the same people we'd arrested only a day earlier. They recognized our vehicles when we arrived and gave us the finger while waving at us. One time a park visitor whom we did not know signaled to us that some people had gone off together to some the bushes beneath the bluff.

Two members of our group—I was not among them—walked there only to witness a teenage girl providing oral sexual pleasure to a teenage boy. They were arrested. In fact, that day those two were the only people we arrested at the park. You throw out the line and pull in whoever takes a bite. Or at least nibbles a little.

Another time we arrested a group of about eight boys and girls—older teenagers—for smoking marijuana. They were loaded on THC to be sure, but other stuff to boot. No mere Buddha beaters get as feisty as this crew became. They fought and screamed and yelled—females included—and we literally dragged some of them to the waiting meat wagon as we used to call the police prisoner conveyance van. For few days there were no lawbreakers. None that we saw, because by this time most of them were regulars who, as previously stated, knew our vehicles and ditched the dope before we got too close. Sometimes they were too high to notice us and they paid the price.

One day we pulled up, got out of our vehicles and a tall slim-but-muscular young man with bright, mid-back length blond hair, stood from where he was sitting at a picnic table and, while shouting one of our names, declared the named person provided donkeys with oral sexual pleasure. Now, he used different words, but you get the idea. We all looked at each other and simultaneously said, "He's under arrest."

We approached and he sucked down the rest of a can of beer he'd been drinking and squared off, as though he were ready to fight. We reached him and laid hands upon him and fight he did. None of us could believe it. We later all agreed we'd never seen an individual knowingly pick a physical fight with a half dozen police officers.

See what drugs and booze will do to you?

Unbelievably, the group of five or six people he'd been enjoying marijuana and beer with joined in to help him. Two of them were teenage girls. Of course, they were all arrested and charged with Battery to a Peace Officer. Only one of them had pot—a small amount—in their possession. We handcuffed them and had to literally drag them to the prisoner wagon. They were all screaming and yelling the whole time.

It gets far more bizarre.

The following morning my partners and I were in municipal court to testify against the—how do you say?—the evil doers. They'd all been processed and released the day before and were all in court on time. The city attorney asked the judge if the group could be tried together, to get things over with more quickly. The judge agreed and allowed the mass trial.

The city attorney was an older, quirky fellow, who no one could believe was actually an attorney. But I digress.

One of our officers was chosen to be the main complaining witness. He stepped to the docket, squared his shoulders and stood tall. Professional. The city attorney quickly instructed the tall blond man, who'd begun the trouble at the park, be the first witness for the defense. The man stood at the defense table.

While pointing at the defendant the quirky city attorney asked the officer: "What did you see that man or hear that man do?"

The officer answered: "He said that Officer fill in the blank—and here is where I will screen the language—'provided oral sex to donkeys'."

The courtroom was full and quiet and many people gasped in shock at the language and imagery it supplied.

"And as far as you know, Officer fill in the blank doesn't do that, does he?"

"Not to my knowledge, no, sir," the officer quickly replied.

The city attorney was a short, spry man, who leaned toward the officer, wearing a stern look on his face. He made a small smile.

I, personally, had a large smile. So did the rest of my partners, where we all stood behind the testifying officer. The fill in the blank officer hung his head.

At first, the courtroom went silent. An instant later it burst with the sound of high pitched, uncontrolled laughter. The defendants standing at their desk doubled over with laughter.

The judge then said loudly into his microphone that all such activity should cease immediately, which it kind of sort of did. In a way. A little bit.

The questioning continued, as did bits and pieces of laughter. The defendant was found guilty on all charges. The judge poignantly asked the young man, "Why did you say that to the officer?"

"Because I don't like him," the just convicted man replied.

The simple truth about human disaffection was explained in words spoken by an eighteen-year-old drunken, drug addict who openly picked fist fights with the police.

The judge rapped his gavel. "Next case," he said.

# TWENTY-THREE
## *King Baner*

The detectives had put the murder in the cold case file some months earlier. There had been no evidence whatsoever: no witnesses, forensics, and no suspects. The victim was an elderly woman who owned a grocery store in what had slowly—but surely—become a bad part of town. She'd been murdered shortly after the store had closed for the evening and she was apparently in the process of locking up.

She'd been found dead on a stairway leading to the basement a few hours after her daughter had made her routine nighttime call to make sure Mom was okay. After too many no answers, the daughter called the police, who investigated and discovered the crime. All of the routine investigative procedures had been completed that night.

Officers who interviewed the victim's daughter said she'd flashed between hysterical crying and screaming anger. She'd been telling her mother to sell the damn place and get the hell out of that criminal neighborhood for years. And now the nightmare had happened. Everyone had predicted it: she'd be a crime victim or maybe even end up dead if she didn't leave.

The killer(s) had been nasty. The dead woman had incurred a fractured skull, had poured out some thick gouts of blood while she tumbled and rolled to the bottom step in the stairwell and then died. Her upper dentures had been knocked out of her mouth during the beating and lay on the step next to her.

Some people in the neighborhood knew her; many did not. A lot of people had moved out over the years and many of those who'd replaced them entered what was a mixed and rapidly deteriorating business and home area of Milwaukee. Most did not shop in her store. It was no longer the cozy, homeland kind of place it had been for generations. What made things worse was she was not the first veteran of the neighborhood's small businesses to be murdered on their the premises.

The warnings were clear and present, but so was the stubbornness.

But there had been a break in the case. A young man with an already bad criminal record was arrested for a crime at another location and was facing serious jail time. Same old story told thousands of times a day across the country. He said a dude from the 'hood had bragged and laughed about how some old lady tried to interrupt his breaking in to her store and he had to smack her one. He quickly left after she fell down the stairs and the next day he learned that she was dead.

Just another occurrence involving young members of local street gangs. Meant nothing to anyone, until the young man now caught needed leverage to help him avoid a lengthy prison term. Another old game played in horrible, crime ridden neighborhoods: murder don't mean nothin' until handing over the information to the police can do you some good.

Detectives and uniformed back up officers went to the home of the named suspect in the murder of the old woman. They found him. He laughed when they told him why they were arresting him. Some whining snitch made up a lie about him, he said while chortling. An officer accompanied him to his room so he could get dressed, while other officers in the living room talked about the case. One of them mentioned the dentures found lying next to the victim's body.

"I remember those," the prisoner muttered quietly—undoubtedly thinking it was only to himself. The officer standing near him noted the remark and told the detectives who'd been assigned to interrogate the suspect. He laughed and denied saying it, but the detectives told the officer to file a report. They'd make it an official part of the investigation. During the interrogation the suspect volunteered more than once to take a lie detector test. He admitted nothing and did not ask for an attorney.

The following morning the D.A. assigned to the case stated the "I remember those" statement by the defendant to the officer regarding the dentures was one-on-one hearsay and he simply could not go to trial with that alone. He'd hold off on the charges if the defendant made good on his offer to take a polygraph exam. Maybe more information would come in during the waiting period. When the D.A. inquired, the defendant laughed and said, "Hell, yeah." The D.A. directed him to Public Defenders office to get a community funded lawyer who would help him make the arrangements .

The D.A. told the officers something they'd already known: even if the defendant failed the exam, he still wouldn't file any charges. Lie detector results are inadmissible in court; they cannot be presented as evidence to the jury. While feeling outraged, the officers also shrugged. They knew the score. The D.A., himself being deeply disappointed, commiserated with the cops. The story goes that he and two of the investigating detectives went out drinking that night. Got hammered. Hammered good. I don't know if that's true, but it's possible.

Many so-called cold cases have that anchor holding the case in place. *We know he did it but we can't prove it.* Into the cold file it goes, most of them forever.

Being a homicide detective has its drawbacks.

I've heard it said that being a cop on any level sucks. Hell, I've said it. And it's crap like this that provokes you.

The sneering killer punk actually lived up to his word and submitted to the polygraph. He passed. It was later reported that he'd taken more than one lie detector before this one, had passed even though he'd been guilty and bragged to his buds in the neighborhood. The D.A. and the cops laughed, knowing things would go no further. Sociopaths have long been known to be able to pass polygraph exams. If a person doesn't care or feel anxiety when they lie, the needle won't move. A normal person will make the needle jump off the page, in a manner of speaking, but the sickos won't make it budge.

The detectives who went through all of this went on with their lives. Wasn't the first time a slam-dunk bad guy had beat the system and it wouldn't be the last. And we'd all laugh things like this off and make extremely insensitive remarks. It's a well-known means of defense.

But no one ever joked with the two detectives about this case. That poor, defenseless old woman, whom everyone loved. The weeping daughter with a broken heart, made worse by knowing the murdering gang member, who had later become a pimp and a drug dealer, was living like royalty. That he was admired and even revered by his fellows for beating the murder rap.

Dark faces with scalding stares would confront anyone joking about *that* one in front of the investigating detectives.

Almost two years later a group of burglars were arrested for committing more than one hundred burglaries. It meant one man living in the lap of criminal luxury was about to be in serious trouble. Two of the burglars who were cooperating had been with the man who'd smashed the head of the old woman two years earlier. They gave detailed confessions, which included information that had never been made public. Like the dentures lying next to the dead woman's body. Like naming the man who had done it.

It was over for him.

One of the original investigating detectives of the murder happened to be working the day the co-defendants snitched off the Main Man. The detective was taken off of a different assignment and brought along to make the arrest of the soon-to-be doing life in prison without parole guilty man.

The detective later said it was the best day of his career; one of the best days of his life.

Someone said the arrested man had fought with the detective who first laid hands on him when the arrest was made and that he had a few bumps on his head and face. None of us were surprised. Murderers always fight with the cops who arrest them—as the old saying goes.

He was later convicted of the crime. One of the city's most notorious, royalty like gang leaders, went from a glittering pot of gold to sharing space with a stinking, stainless-steel toilet sitting two feet from his prison cot. This happened in the early 1980s. Several years ago, long after I'd retired, I was told that he'd died in prison and his unclaimed remains were cremated and disposed of in the usual manner on the prison grounds.

# TWENTY-FOUR
## *99.9%*

A gruesome murder provided many weeks of *Milwaukee Journal* headlines also created much more than the description of a crime; an acknowledgment of the fear rippling through the city. International intrigue eventually grew from the violence and the remains of a teenage girl who lay dead in a wooded area of a small park on the city's northwest side. A beautiful, athletic, all-around high achieving young woman was sexually assaulted and strangled. Ordinarily, there would be local news reporting from the scene and some follow up and the family would gather and grieve. That occurred in the case to which I am referencing. And of course everyone hoped that the killer would be located and on his way to prison. The heinous crime was never quite solved. I hedge by using the qualifying "quite" word because, after several years, the perp was known and in prison, but for other crimes. We think. We're, like, 99.9% certain he committed the murder. If it sounds as if there had been problems for the legal community—the world-wide legal community—it is no coincidence.

How would they say it nowadays? There were problems times infinity? Whatever, that is how I'm saying it.

The murder occurred in July, 1979. The victim and all others involved, whatever their part, will not be named. But there are still many people who remember the case. I certainly do since I had a part—a very small part—in investigating the matter.

A high-ranking officer of the Milwaukee Police Department had, coincidentally, been a good friend of the victim's father. The victim had been missing for three days and her parents said that when she had been five minutes late getting home from a bicycle ride, they knew "something dreadful had happened." The mother was a basket case, the father was holding on.

Then came the report of the body being found, less than one half mile from her home and the father immediately went to the scene. The police were there and the scene was sealed off, but the father wanted to see his daughter's remains, anyway. That's what always goes on. And sealed off means no one but those with explicit authority can enter, including the closest relatives.

The high-ranking officer arrived and spoke with his friend, the girl's father, and immediately made a poor decision. He allowed the father to see the remains, as they were found, in the small park forest.

Side note: I saw photos of the victim taken almost immediately after she was found, before the scene was processed. They horrified the most experienced and hard-nosed homicide detectives there are. They were as shocking and grotesque as those that were taken at Nazi war camps.

Imagine how the sight affected her father.

It was literally the end of his mental well-being; the beginning of a lifetime of steadily progressing mental derangement.

The high-ranking officer thoughtlessly figured he was doing his buddy an insider favor.

He was wrong.

That part of this story needs no further commentary. One can imagine the fallout for many people, in different ways and on different levels.

There were no suspects; all possibilities were

examined and there was absolutely nothing. There were no clues. There was merely the victim's remains and her bicycle, which the killer had flung up into some tree branches. A few days later her tennis shoe and some underwear were located in an open sewer pipe on the park grounds.

Being a brand new major crimes detective, I was more-or-less a gopher for the veterans. But I was aware of and saw everything. We did follow up for many months after.

What's about international intrigue, you may be wondering?

It starts like this. Less than a year earlier a woman jogging in a park in the Milwaukee suburb of Greenfield, which is on the other side of the city, had been strangled and left in some bushes. That was the extent of the crime—no removal of clothing or sexual assault. One who commits rape and then kills is considered to be in a more twisted psychological area—not that murdering a stranger in a park isn't savage enough on its own. But sexual assault is a decidedly, more harsh, more complex thrown in with the premeditated murder of a stranger.

But it was all our lead detectives had, so they looked into the Greenfield Police Department's investigation. A couple names of possible suspects had been thrown around, mostly out of desperation and as a common tactic to keep the news media and the people living in the nearby area a sense that their police are doing their job. Which they are, by the way. The cases were not related.

A possible witness eventually came forward. He'd seen a young man in the park around the time the victim had been on her bike ride. The witness viewed suspect photos in the Detective Bureau, with no success.

Meanwhile, the dead girl's father grew frustrated and

hired a private detective to get involved with the investigation. And that's where the bizarre twist began.

The PI was pretty wealthy, lived in a posh neighborhood and had a reputation as an extremely hard worker who had exposed a fair number of insurance frauds and the like.

It was soon to be learned that he did not know the difference between civil and criminal investigations.

Eyewitnesses in criminal matters must view a line-up of four or five people and then successfully identify the person whom they saw committing whatever act is being investigated. A photo lineup uses photos of people casting the same pose in each picture. As everyone is aware, an artist's sketch can be used as a look-out device for the police to possibly find a photo or person who closely matches and to show the public, so they might be able to name someone. Such scenarios have famously paid off through the generations.

An investigator does not take a single photo or drawing to a possible eyewitness, have said witness say "That's the guy!" and then think they can use that "identification" as evidence to get a warrant. Said investigator also does not go to his buddies at the city's main newspaper and have them print an above-the-fold copy of said drawing on the front page of the newspaper with the declaration:"This is the suspect!"

The reasons? It is considered prejudicial to show a single photo to a witness and it is therefore not admissible in court. It also messes up further use of the photo in the investigation. Having the newspaper print the drawing of what some people—not necessarily the police—believe is the perp also destroys the credibility of the drawing for purposes of use in a trial. This is a fundamental rule that law enforcement officials, attorneys and judges all know well.

Gets better.

The chief of police does not order the destruction of the police copy of the drawing, simply because he's angry about the way it was misused. Said chief should not need a lieutenant explain to him the reasons why, like the defense has a right to see the drawing and you can lose the case if you destroyed it. The explanation was necessary in this case. I will allow the information I've cited to stand alone, without discussion or opinion attached.

Gets better.

One of the names the Greenfield police came up with appeared in the army roster of a troop in Germany. The young man had enlisted in the army shortly after the rape-murder of the young girl on the city's north side. The new soldier had been stationed in Europe after basic training. The soldier was arrested in Germany for molesting a woman in a bar.

The Milwaukee District Attorney said, "That's all we got," and two Milwaukee detective were sent to Germany to interview the soldier-molester. He was questioned and denied everything about the Milwaukee murders. Our detectives—two of the best I ever saw—came back saying with certainty, "This is our guy!"

No proof, but these guys know their killers and rapists. The soldier-molester was dishonorably discharged and sent back to the States. A short while later he was arrested in Chicago for the rape-murder of a woman in a park. He's a slam-dunk, cold turkey, hanging upside down on a hook in a slaughterhouse. Our detectives go to Chicago to interview him. His attorney says the murder-rapist will only talk if he gets a deal. You mean, he did our Milwaukee rapes and murders, our guys ask his attorney? The attorney responds with a coy smile and raises his eyebrows.

The suspect tells his attorney: no deal in the Milwaukee cases, no confession. He'll take his chances in Chicago. He lost.

Our D.A.—and everyone else in the legal community—says that's as close as we're ever gonna get. The soldier-rapist-murderer dude is doing life without parole in Illinois. Our case in Milwaukee is, and will remain, 99.9% closed.

Addendum: the father of the Milwaukee victim deteriorated badly and did several rehabilitation stints in psychiatric wards. The word was that he'd never recovered. He passed away a few years ago.

# TWENTY-FIVE
## *Get Used to It*

The first day I was assigned to work a one man police squad was...different. I was anxious, as all cops are under these conditions. But my anxiety gave way to a sort of bravado. I was young. What did I know?

My assignment was in the very quiet south side of Milwaukee The homes are gorgeous, mostly built in the first half of the 20th century. Their design was based on the Old World-European style, which populate most large American cities to this day.

Down-to-Earth type people dominated the area. There were some rundown homes gathered in the areas where the first family businesses were opened. Only a few were of the slum category. On this fine autumn day I started by driving the particular route I'd seen veterans follow when I was the passenger in two officer assignments in the area. They knew the so-called hot spots. But this was the cities 2nd Precinct, after all. It was mostly crime free.

"Squad twenty-seven" came through the police radio. It was my squad number and the dispatcher was calling to give me my first assignment of the day. There'd been a report that some juveniles were throwing things out of a second story window. It was in a shanty home area and considered routine.

When I arrived there was no one around. The residence to which I'd been sent was a small, white two-story building. The front door, which was immediately adjacent to the sidewalk in front, stood wide open. I called out and received no answer. I slowly entered, continuing to ask if anyone was home.

I cautiously stepped inside and continued calling out. Finally, a young boy—later determined to be eleven years old—with long, jet black hair, appeared at the top of the stairs.

"Is something wrong?" he asked anxiously, in a pre-pubescent, high-pitched male voice.

He was obviously the kid who was throwing stuff out of the window and he knew someone had called the cops. It was laughably obvious and one could feel his angst while he continued trying to play innocent. New guy though I was, I felt confident I'd quickly solve the mystery.

He provided his name and birth date without hesitation. He said his mother should be in the kitchen downstairs, at the back of the house. He came down the steps and went to get her. The atmosphere grew more calm.

The boy's mother came out to the hallway. She was extremely short and plump and wore a light-colored, full-length house dress. She looked utterly perplexed while looking me up and down. She was upset, to say the least. I would even say she was a bit frightened. I sensed she spoke only broken English. Comparing her to other foreigners living in the area, I guessed that she was an immigrant from Central Europe.

The boy stood next to her. I explained the reason why I was sent. Her quizzical look remained. The boy started off by translating what I was saying. She relaxed a bit and looked at me with anticipation.

After a few moments of the boy playing interpreter, the woman began to speak for herself in very poor English. She'd been cooking and cleaning in the kitchen. Before that she had done laundry in the basement. Her son had a couple of friends over and they were laughing and playing in the living room. They ran up and down the stairs leading to the second floor, where her son's bedroom was.

After explaining the details of the complaint, the boy quickly denied throwing anything out the window. He volunteered to take me into the front room and up to his bedroom to show how everything was neat and in order.

I had no doubt that he was lying. He and his buddies had indeed been throwing something out the window when they went upstairs, mostly likely to his bedroom. They had upset at least one neighbor, who called the cops. He had the look of a kid who would automatically deny his actions. His mom, a teacher, a cop.

Having a foreign mother most probably gave him an advantage when it came to getting away with naughty things.

The kid shrugged, his mother smiled and winked—yeah, she was flirting—and I left. About ten minutes later the dispatcher called me again. The same anonymous person called and complained that the cop who was just there didn't do anything about their complaint. How come? And the kids buddies, who'd left just before I'd arrived, had already returned.

I returned.

This time the original young boy and two others about his age were standing outside the house, laughing. When they saw me pull up, they quickly moved toward the front door of the house.

The boy who lived there entered the front door. The two boys stopped when I called out. They shrugged when I told them why I was there. One of them said, "It was just some paper airplanes."

So, the boy who lived there had in fact lied. I said I had to talk to his mother.

Both boys became uneasy, and one of them asked if I could just let it go, which surprised me. There was a strange, anxious tone in his voice.

I went to the open door and called out. The boy and his mother appeared in the hallway. It was eerily quiet. The boy walked up to me, head down and handed me some crumpled pieces of paper. Paper airplanes! He turned and went back to once again stand next to his mother. His mother remained silent and appeared to be confused.

"Here," I said, showing her the paper airplanes. I told her I'd been called back to her house, that neighbors want her son to go to jail. A typical exaggeration by a cop to get someone's attention. The mother suddenly looked at her son and began screaming at him in a foreign language. I was shocked. She stopped screaming, smiled weakly at me and signaled that I could leave. She'd gotten it.

Once outside I heard a loud slapping sound. She'd obviously struck the boy. She began screaming again. He began crying. I stopped and waited. Some parents hit their kids. I waited a while longer and there were no more hitting sounds. With no complaining witness and no signs—proof—that she'd hurt him unreasonably, I had no choice but to leave.

Not long after I heard "Squad twenty-seven" on the dispatch speaker. When I answered he said, "Return to your previous assignment. There's a battery complaint."

Not surprised, I answered the dispatcher and headed back, yet again.

"Squad two will join squad twenty-seven," I quickly heard on the radio. "I know what this is about."

Squad two was my patrol sergeant. Uh oh. Had I done something wrong?

We arrived at the same time. We exchanged salutes but no words were spoken. He pounded on the door.

There was no answer. The same neighbor approached us.

"Wow," he said, "she was strappin' that boy good."

"Did you see it?" the sergeant asked.

"No, just heard it."

The sergeant clenched his jaw and deeply knit his brow. He slammed his fist on the door several times. There was no answer.

"They still in there?" he asked the neighbor.

"Far as I know."

The sergeant had regained control and looked me dead in the eye.

"Take your turn," he said to me.

Knowing what he meant, I pounded on the door. There was no answer. No sound at all from inside the home.

"Thanks for your concern," he said to the neighbor and began walking away. I followed

"Nothin' you can do?" the neighbor called to us. "This ain't the first time."

The sergeant stopped, as did I.

He held up one hand and touched the forefinger. "Did you see anything? Anything at all? Did the boy come outside with injuries? *Anything*?"

"No," the man replied in a soft voice.

The sergeant and I walked away.

When we reached an area where no one else could hear us, he stopped and said, "Whadaya think, kid? Should we break down the door and grab everyone and see if the kid has any marks on his body? Put handcuffs on the mother and take her with us?"

I didn't hesitate. "We can't," I said. "Don't have enough."

"We know about this woman," the sergeant said as we started walking again. "The kid won't make a complaint; no one's seen any injuries that we can prove

151

he got from his mom. Fun, huh?" he said with a strong edge of irony in his tone.

I said nothing.

"Get used to it, copper," he said.

# TWENTY-SIX
*Nurse Help*

After a few years working in the Detective Bureau I was among those who had a reputation for being able to do the job. I was still working in the so-called general duty section, where we were men and women for all seasons, as the old saying goes. We investigated every kind of felony. We mostly kept track of burglaries in our assigned areas, but we also investigated many armed robberies and homicides.

There were three detectives assigned to each unit to cover the off days and always have two people working a shift. That is standard procedure in most major city police departments. Of course, we got to know each other well and became friends. The three of us often socialized with our families. Normal stuff.

But we were cops, and normal stuff only lasted so long in our lives as partners. One of my partners was married to a registered nurse who worked at a local hospital. We all had young children and got along fine. Actually, boring stuff and Normal Rockwell would have slobbered all over us. Then he could have done a portrait of our families.

All three of us collectively had many years of service in the most crime filled areas of the city. So, we were seasoned veterans. But there is some seasoning that comes upon you that you would never have guessed. It's called life, but those certain unexpected life experiences never fail to at least shock, if they do real damage.

When the result of the unexpected event is a large,

above-the-fold headline on the front page of the local newspaper, it certainly is at least a big-ass deal. How much damage there is; sometimes you have to wait to see.

Early in the evening of one routine work day, my partner and I were in the detective assembly area, checking some reports. Without being aware of it, my partner had stepped away from our desk. I continued studying a report. A short while late my partner approached and said we had an assignment and to meet in the garage at our squad. Nothing unusual about that.

Once in the car my partner said that while I was enjoying reading police reports, he'd been called to the side by the sift commander who told him our third partner, who was on his day off, had a problem. We were going to his house to speak with he and his wife, the nurse. He smiled.

"You're not gonna like this," he said, or words to that effect.

A greasy, queasy, anxious—that's right, all three at the same time—feeling quickly grew within me. I looked at him and he had the strangest look. A combination of a smirk and a frown. He was a serious kind of guy and I felt that we were headed into a *Twilight Zone* kind of thing.

I was right.

I'll never forget the commotion that began and grew in my guts and the other usual and customary inner parts. Our partner had called the shift commander to tell him a story. It was a story about his wife and an incident—actually several incidents—that had occurred at the hospital where she worked.

She and several other nurses were good friends and would go out for cocktails from time to time. One night they asked and she said she was tired; she didn't want to go. One of her nurse mates grabbed her hard by the arm and said in her ear, "You're going. We've got something to tell you." She went.

She nervously drove to their usual nightclub and was the last one to arrive. The other women wore stone-like expressions. As she went to sit at their booth, another of their fellow nurses joined them. He was male, about thirty years old. She said he was a good nurse and a nice guy. A bit of a loner, but okay.

He leaned in and said to our partner's wife that the other women all knew what he was about to say.

"I pulled the plug on an old lady in a coma last week. She died."

Our partner's wife felt sick and did not want to be there. But the other women knew about the event first and decided they all needed to know. They told the male nurse of their meeting and he said he'd join them. Said he wanted to explain his side of the story.

Of course, there was only one story: the man had cut of the oxygen to a patient, without her consent and she then died. It's called murder. The women had tried to explain that to him, but he refused to get it. They hoped our partner's wife, being married to a homicide detective, might be able to better explain how much trouble he was in.

He refused to catch on and they all left. The next day, we were sent to our other partner's house to take a statement from his wife.

"What about conflict of interest?" I cried.

"It would only be suggested in this case. The bosses talked it over and it will not jeopardize the case against the nurse who actually pulled the plug." He went on to say the other women had all given statements to other detectives and they would arrest the accused nurse the following day, after all of the statements were completed and typed up.

I didn't like it. My partner didn't like it. Our third

partner said that after thinking it all through, he didn't care. All he cared about was that his wife wasn't involved with the death.

# TWENTY-SEVEN
## Chi Town

It had been a busy stretch. An immediate assignment right out of the barn, as we used to say virtually every day. At 4:00 p.m. we'd be running to the squad straight from roll call. Better this than getting some over-the-hill day shift detective's meaningless follow up, one of my partners used to say.

And he was right. Nothing worse than finishing someone else's work because they wanted to go home on time or because they couldn't figure it out themselves. So off to the wild blue we went, laughing at the other guys who had to sit and listen to someone tell them how to finish their assignment.

"This one's a little different," our lieutenant said as he explained the assignment to us while we sat in his office. "Information came in that a known burglar has been hiding out at the house you're going to." It was also a drug house, where they sold crack. Those particular users were out shopping twenty-four hours a day, so the house often had a lot of people there.

He told us to take some district squads with us to clearly overwhelm anyone who thought about resisting our visit.

"What's his name?" my partner asked about the man we were trying to locate.

No name, only a description, we were told. But the informant was one of the best the narcotics squad had and he'd told the narcs the burglar was definitely there. The informant had just bought some and the dude was sitting in the living room, talking about being wanted on a warrant.

We arranged for four additional uniformed officers to meet with us a short distance from the house we were going to. We told the officers all that we knew and one of them wisely said, "So, we'll basically be searching and getting ID from everyone there."

No one answered. It was true and it was just business as usual. Defense attorneys had long been claiming the police would make up a story about some anonymous informant giving us this information just so we could roust a house full of people we didn't like. I personally explained many times to defense lawyers that we would never do such a thing. It would be unethical. It would be outside the law. I don't think any of them believed me.

We all got into our respective squads and drove to the house. My partner and I would go to the rear, along with two uniformed officers, and the other two officers would cover the front. Standard procedure, just a matter of deciding which officers would execute which assignment.

The residence was on the second floor and the people living on the first floor let us in after we knocked. The sound of many fast moving feet emanated from the second floor. Of course, our suspicions were aroused. While explaining our business to a man from the lower residence, we could hear chairs and tables being dragged across either hardwood or linoleum floors up in the second story.

My partner and I pushed past the balking, doubtlessly-hesitating-to-help-the-criminals-upstairs-resident and climbed the rear stairway two steps at a time. We knocked hard on the door. No one answered. We waited a moment, knocked again and this time we announced that we were the police and had business with them.

After a bit of time the door knob turned and the door opened. A young, otherwise unremarkable looking man given the environment, asked if he could help us. He seemed bored and talked and moved slowly.

I stepped inside the room with the two uniformed officers. My partner took the young man who'd answered the door into the hallway and closed the door. The room was a kitchen with a bright light overhead and four or five young men sat at an old style chrome and tile kitchen table. They were playing cards. Poker, as I recall. Each had several playing cards in their hands and the rest of the cards and some poker chips sat in the middle of the table.

What fun they were having!

While explaining in minimal terms why we were there, we asked to see their identification. One of them asked if we had probable cause to do what we were doing. I told him we did, a reliable informant had just told us that a felony suspect we were looking for was in the house and we'd gotten there as quickly as we could in the hopes of catching a criminal. I congratulated him for knowing the law so well. I always congratulated suspicious people when they challenged me on search and seizure procedures. The school system was doing its job.

Meanwhile, my partner and the other young man who'd kept out in the hallway were *still* in the hallway. The young men at the table all showed us whatever ID they'd been carrying that day. But they were getting nervous. They were constantly looking at the closed kitchen door.

What could the other detective be talking to him about? They knew it meant trouble for someone—maybe even all of them.

A short while later my partner came into the room with the young man.

"No one say anything!" he quickly said in a loud voice.

The room was quiet.

My partner turned to the young man at his side, pointed randomly at another young man who was sitting at the kitchen table, and asked, "What's his name?"

The young man said nothing because obviously he didn't know.

My partner pointed at another young man at the table and asked, "What is his name?"

Again, no answer.

My partner then pointed at one of the men at the table and asked, "What is this man's name?" He was pointing at the man whom he'd been interviewing in the hallway. The man at the table said nothing.

My partner laughed and said, "I think I've made my point."

"And what point is that, Detective?" one of the officers asking in a most proper and respectful manner.

"It means that nobody knows nuttin'," he said. He laughed again.

He quickly explained that just before we entered we had heard a bunch of footsteps and tables and chairs being dragged across the floor, and then by golly we come in and everyone's sitting quietly at the table, playing a friendly game of poker.

My partner then placed handcuffs on the man he was holding. My partner looked at me, smiled, and said he'd found a pot pipe and a chunk of hashish in the young man's pocket while doing a pat-down search. The others at the table became anxious and began to speak out.

"You ain't arresting me!" one of them shouted. "I showed my license."

"Me, too," another quickly said. "You got a warrant on me?"

We knew that those two were not the suspect we were searching for. In fact, they both voluntarily put their hands above their heads and formed the most innocent looking expressions imaginable on their faces.

After a few deliciously silent moments, the young man sitting at the end of the table stood, turned, and attempted to run into the front room. The two uniformed officers on that side of the table easily captured and restrained him.

"Where do you think you're going?" one of the officers asked while laughing.

The man was obviously quite intoxicated on who-knew-what drugs.

Another of the young men quickly stood. I grabbed him and handcuffed him.

"I ain't tryin' nothin'," he said, or words to that effect.

I told him to just relax, that things were getting out of control. I felt his clinched muscles loosen. It was clear he too was high on some kind of drug. Looking around the table, it was obvious they were all high.

Once they were all properly identified, it turned out there were warrants on all of them. Most of it was petty stuff: shoplifting, unpaid traffic tickets. One of them did have a burglary warrant, but it was from many months earlier—he was not the suspect we were looking for.

We called for a prisoner conveyance and the matter was soon resolved. Except for one detail: we didn't get the guy the informant had described. Or, did we? There'd have to be a lineup of photos shown to the informant and any other witnesses. There was more work to do.

The officers praised my partner for the sweet technique of quickly separating one from the group and after bringing him back into the room, we saw that "nobody knew nuttin'." They were all quickly proved to be liars because they didn't know what the young man had told my partner. They couldn't tell the truth or make off-the-wall alibis since it would jeopardize the other people at the table.

It's fun being a member of or associated with a street gang. We later learned the man who tried to run had been using phony ID for more than a year. After he was fingerprinted at headquarters, he was wanted for a homicide in Chicago.

All in a days' work.

# TWENTY-EIGHT
## *LT*

Thirty years can seem, as the cliché goes, like an eternity. But then so can thirty seconds given the right conditions. Metaphysicians say it's proof that there really is no time, that there are only events. Well, those are muddy waters for us folks stuck in the physical realm. Some predict we'll each come to know the difference; to know the truth. And, really, we all will.

It's just it might not make any difference.

That remark is from the roots of my police experience. Ya gotta always end every serious thing with an offbeat remark, whether it's funny or not. At least in your mind. It gets you by. Sometimes.

I didn't attend one of those events where time does not matter. I heard about it and maybe there's a lesson there. Events don't matter: only the truth does.

And the truth is Lieutenant of Police Lenard Wells spent his final years on the Milwaukee Police Department supervising patrol officers and sergeants on the day shift of a precinct located in a primarily Caucasian neighborhood—Milwaukee's south side. He supervised mostly Caucasian officers.

And the officers loved him. They'd never worked for a police supervisor like him: scary smart, witty, calm, able to do everything as though it were a simple, throw away situation. Even though it wasn't.

And as Lieutenant Wells approached retirement, he considered running for alderman in one of Milwaukee's neighborhood precincts. He'd spent time with department and general city politics, fighting for the exercise of equal rights for everyone, so he was not inexperienced, or naive.

The people at the Second District Day Shift put together a fundraiser for him at a south side tavern owned by a former Milwaukee police officer. It was kept quiet and the tavern was prepared for the party, with signs and you-name-it kinds of promotion for his run for office. A couple of officers said they needed him to drop in as a special guest at the retirement party of an old, good friend of his, that he needed to come straight from work—before he changed from his uniform.

He had no clue about what was to happen.

He entered the tavern and immediately knew he'd been had. About one hundred officers were in attendance, giving ear-splitting shouts of support for the man.

For Lenard Wells

He was a cool cat and kept his composure. For a while. Eventually a detective, who'd been my partner at the time and who had worked for Lenard as a patrol officer when Lenard was a sergeant, sidled up to him where he sat in a booth, in his place of honor. The music was blaring, the alcohol was flowing and the sheer joy in the atmosphere was immeasurable.

"Lenny," the detective said. "You came to Milwaukee as a poor, young black boy in the 1960s. Look what happened. You finished your college education, became a cop who'd earned the hushed, reverent words of his peers, was promoted to the rank of Lieutenant, in charge of a district dominated by white people. At a police station dominated by white cops. Look around. Look how you are worshiped by these guys, who would like to see you help make laws to run Milwaukee. What do you think the odds were on that, back when you first came to live here."

By the time the detective finished, long streaks of tears were sliding down Lenard's cheeks. His lips quivered. He was speechless. But he did not lose control. He looked at the detective, shook his head and then looked down.

It was a timeless event. A moment that had no business playing out in the 1990s, according to all the social experts. But it stills beats fresh in my heart, and I know it does so in Lenard Wells' heart.

He did not win his race. He finished his time with the department and moved back to Missouri to live with his core family. He'd single handedly wiped out and put in prison a murderous gang of drug dealers and pimps and then nonchalantly provided supervision for the rest of us.


One day after I'd retired from the force, my twenty-year-old son called and said, "Hey, Dad, guess who's teaching me how to be a cop!?" He'd enrolled in the police science course at a local college, and had been changing courses and instructors.

I had no clue.

"Lenard Wells!" he cried out. "Your old partner on the Vice Squad. Says you personally saved his life five times."

If I had been drinking a beverage, I'd have spit it from here to the moon.

I quickly gathered my wits.

"It was six times, son."

After a medium length pause, he said, "Do cops ever stop joking around like this?"

"No."

My son went on from that moment more than fifteen years ago to actually become a Milwaukee police officer and then—a Milwaukee Police Sergeant. He supervises officers in the same morose neighborhoods that I'd roamed during my time on the force.

It's dangerous and scary work in an area like that, but at least it isn't undercover.

# TWENTY-NINE
## *The FBI*

Few things are more demeaning to a modern day law enforcement officer than being called a "Wyatt Earp." Depending on the circumstances, the officer will laugh it off or be a bit insulted. This is not new—it has long been a rib-tickler for cops—but of course sometimes it's true. When an individual cop steps outside the law, he/she must face appropriate consequences. There is compelling information that the OK Corral incident and follow-up was not properly handled. Unauthorized gun slinging ruled the day.

The gunfight at the OK Corral was a watershed moment for America's police type authorities. A well-respected, even revered man, and his gang had marched off and killed some bad guys they'd been having trouble with for a while. Earp was vindicated, and I'm not going to re-analyze the investigation and succeeding court room proceedings, but questions were raised that resonate to this day. Actually, police procedures were looked at hard by upstanding, qualified people with first class resumes and some favorite sons got off the hook, but things had to get started somehow.

The USA was quickly growing in all respects and by the 20th century many previously inconceivable and wonderful inventions had been introduced. Ways of improving life were coming into existence by the day. Everyone had to change, like it or not. Some caught on quickly and changed as needed, others didn't care and kept on a goin' like the old days. They ended being dragged into changing.

At the top of the list were criminal and civil laws; behavior was being checked and balanced. The laws changed and new ones were quickly added, as needed. The manner and legitimacy of those changes will forever be debated. Declarations stamped in black and white onto paper are one thing. Human behavior is another.

That takes us from October of 1883, the time of the OK Corral episode, to August of 1974, the time of another, lesser-known event occurring between Chicago and Milwaukee. A headline dominating splash was, technically at least, more of a doozy than the 19th century deal in the Arizona desert.

The course of life caused law enforcement and the courts to change—some say improve, others claim not so much—in mind bending ways. Constables On Patrol—cops—were better and more reliably trained and held accountable for inappropriate actions. Most of the time, to be certain.

Wyatt Earp's day was a fuzzy—even cozy in some ways—memory.

We can recount all the events and reasons for upgrades throughout the ages. We can name all the different law enforcement—and even include the military a bit—and the reasons for all the specialized, sophisticated training they've undergone. It's a compelling, entertaining story. But you have to pay particular attention to America's Big Dog in the law enforcement field during the ultimate modernization: The FBI. And the guy who really made the organization famous: J. Edgar Hoover.

In some important ways, J. Edgar ran the entire country and was determined to do everything his way. In secret, if he so desired. Even the President of the United States could just buzz off. Literally. The whole

Kennedy family could tell you stories, if they were still around.

It's even been said J. Edgar continued running the agency for years after his death and knee-jerk worshipers of the man did everything they could to make everyone pretend as if he was still alive. This story directly from a gleefully giggling FBI agent I'd come in contact with as a police detective.

This, however, is a story from the FBI's deep, dark past—1974 is deep and dark, is it not?—not current operations. The changes needed were quickly recognized and have been remarkable and the cooperation between the Feds and the locals is almost unrecognizable with its improvements.

Yes, J. Edgar had passed away two years before the investigation I'm about to describe, but it still didn't make much difference. As you may have guessed, I'm saying that in some ways, it was as though Wyatt Earp was *also* still alive. At least in spirit and his sneering, presumptuous attitude. Heavy language, I know, but I was there. And many of my fellow surviving officers would back me up.

In 1974 a man named Jacob Peter Cohen committed a robbery in Chicago and in the process he shot and killed two Chicago police officers. He escaped from the scene and fled to Milwaukee. Now, bank robberies are the FBI's "thing" and perpetrators crossing state lines add more weight to the FBI's interest and authority.

The suspect arrived at a neighborhood on Milwaukee's east side and hid out in a residence for about a day. But the investigation could not have been more intense. It was strongly assisted by citizens who'd heard and read reports about the incident. Mr. Cohen was located and the information was turned over to the law enforcement authorities.

And *that's* where things went horribly wrong.

The FBI's sources had come through for them. That was all that mattered. It was a J. Edgar moment, if there ever was one—J. Edgar was dead? Ha!

A couple of the Milwaukee agents were concerned it was time to saddle up and go get a bad guy. It was later determined they had virtually no training how to approach and arrest a monstrous, psychopathic murderer of police officers who was holing up and prepared to defend himself to the death. A couple of guys in suits, ties and pistols on their hips were enough to do the job. Sorry, but that describes the 1974 Milwaukee group of FBI agents.

Perhaps someone at the office—the commanding officer?—could have thought to send more people, or even include the Milwaukee Police Department, before heading out to the OK Corral—oops! I mean the small east side apartment in which Mr. Cohen was hiding.

In retrospect, a claim was allegedly made that the MPD had first been notified by the FBI, but it was never verified.

The small group of agents went to the apartment and walked single file up a narrow, outdoor stairway leading to Mr. Cohen's hideout. But Mr. Cohen was a crafty criminal; he saw them coming and opened the door to shoot at them.

Apparently taken by surprise, the agents froze in place and one of them was shot in the mid-section. While seriously wounded, thankfully he survived his injury.

Mr. Cohen managed to flee, ran a few blocks and forced himself into the home of a local attorney, where his three underage children were. Alone. Mr. Cohen took them hostage and in the intensely hysterical moment actually spoke with someone at a local radio station demanding a vehicle for his escape. More than one hundred people, mostly officers and some curious citizens, flooded the neighborhood. During the initial rush, Mr. Cohen saw and shot a Milwaukee Police Detective in the leg—he, too, survived. The police Tactical Squad, armed with rifles and all other manner of high-grade equipment and weaponry, zeroed in on the place.

A car was located and a savvy police officer who knew about car engines manipulated said engine so it would go no faster than thirty miles per hour.

The car was brought to the house; the cop killer came out holding a gun to the head of a child hostage and walked toward the car. The young boy slipped away from the murderer's grasp and ran, and said murderer was instantly shot to death by the Tac Squad police officers.

The incident was given live, nationwide radio and TV coverage, while it was still in progress.

Someone quickly asked, "Why didn't the FBI agents call the MPD before approaching Jacob Peter Cohen?"

Another asked, "Why were the agents not equipped with heavier assault equipment and armored protection?"

There were a lot more. Rumor was the MPD chief's office and the 1974 version of J. Edgar Hoover's office rumbled, shook, and nearly fell to pieces while said commanders discussed the FBI's handling of the matter.

I wasn't there.

Later that year the head agent of the Milwaukee's FBI chapter was presented by the U.S. government with a meritorious service award for his brave actions during the capture of Jacob Peter Cohen.

Wyatt Earp and J. Edgar Hoover would have been proud.

# ACKNOWLEDGMENTS

I would like to thank Jon Jordan for allowing me to post the *Tales from the Blue Line* articles on the *Crimespree Magazine* blog. His help in promoting this book is incalculable.

## ABOUT THE AUTHOR

Rob Riley lives with his wife Mary Lynne in SE Wisconsin. He spent thirty-two years as a Milwaukee police officer—seven years working undercover on the narcotics squad, twenty-two years as a major crimes detective. Writing and reading have been his lifelong passions, and he began writing short stories more than thirty years ago. Police work provided both the inspiration and the insight for writing PI crime mystery novels. His previous novel, Portrait of Murder, won a Lovey award at the Love Is Murder crime mystery conference in Chicago, Illinois in 2013. Dead Last is the second in the ongoing Jack Blanchard PI mystery series. A third novel has been completed, and additional works are in progress.

www.robrileysnovels.net.

OTHER TITLES FROM DOWN AND OUT BOOKS

*See www.DownAndOutBooks.com for complete list*

By Anonymous-9
*Bite Hard*

By J.L. Abramo
*Catching Water in a Net*
*Clutching at Straws*
*Counting to Infinity*
*Gravesend*
*Chasing Charlie Chan*
*Circling the Runway*

By Trey R. Barker
*2,000 Miles to Open Road*
*Exit Blood*
*Death is Not Forever*

By Richard Barre
*The Innocents*
*Bearing Secrets*
*Christmas Stories*
*The Ghosts of Morning*
*Blackheart Highway*
*Burning Moon*
*Echo Bay*
*Lost*

By Eric Beetner and
JB Kohl
*Over Their Heads* (*)

By Eric Beetner and
Frank Scalise
*The Backlist* (*)

By Rob Brunet
*Stinking Rich*
By Dana Cameron (editor)
*Murder at the Beach:*
*Bouchercon Anthology 2014*

By Stacey Cochran
*Eddie & Sunny*

By Mark Coggins
*No Hard Feelings* (*)

By Tom Crowley
*Vipers Tail*
*Murder in the Slaughterhouse*

By Frank De Blase
*Pine Box for a Pin-Up*
*Busted Valentines and Other*
*Dark Delights*

By Les Edgerton
*The Genuine, Imitation, Plastic*
*Kidnapping*

By A.C. Frieden
*Tranquility Denied*
*The Serpent's Game*
*The Pyongyang Option* (*)

By Jack Getze
*Big Numbers*
*Big Money*
*Big Mojo*
*Big Shoes* (*)

*(*)—Coming Soon*

OTHER TITLES FROM DOWN AND OUT BOOKS

*See www.DownAndOutBooks.com for complete list*

By Richard Godwin
*Wrong Crowd* (*)

By William Hastings (editor)
*Stray Dogs: Writing from the
Other America*

By Matt Hilton
*No Going Back*
*Rules of Honor* (*)
*The Lawless Kind* (*)

By Darrel James,
Linda O. Johnston &
Tammy Kaehler (editors)
*Last Exit to Murder*

By David Housewright &
Renée Valois
*The Devil and the Diva*

By David Housewright
*Finders Keepers*
*Full House*

By Jon & Ruth Jordan (editors)
*Murder and Mayhem in
Muskego*
*Cooking with Crimespree*

By Andrew McAleer & Paul D.
Marks (editors)
*Coast to Coast* (*)

By Bill Moody
*Czechmate*

*The Man in Red Square*
*Solo Hand*
*The Death of a Tenor Man*
*The Sound of the Trumpet*
*Bird Lives!*

By Gary Phillips
*The Perpetrators*
*Scoundrels* (Editor)
*Treacherous*

By Robert J. Randisi
*Upon My Soul*
*Souls of the Dead*
*Envy the Dead* (*)

By Ryan Sayles
*The Subtle Art of Brutality* (*)
*Warpath* (*)

By Anthony Neil Smith
*Worm*

By Liam Sweeny
*Welcome Back, Jack* (*)

By Lono Waiwaiole
*Wiley's Lament*
*Wiley's Shuffle*
*Wiley's Refrain*
*Dark Paradise*

By Vincent Zandri
*Moonlight Weeps*

*(*)—Coming Soon*

Proof

41727038R00113

Made in the USA
Charleston, SC
06 May 2015